D1117596

# THE ELEMENTS OF
# ORGANIC GARDENING

## HIGHGROVE   CLARENCE HOUSE   BIRKHALL

## HRH THE PRINCE OF WALES
### WITH STEPHANIE DONALDSON

PHOTOGRAPHY BY ANDREW LAWSON
ADDITIONAL PHOTOGRAPHY BY DAVID ROWLEY

WITHDRAWN

LONDON

PUBLIC LIBRARY

AND

ART MUSEUM

WEIDENFELD & NICOLSON

LONDON PUBLIC LIBRARY

# Contents

# I  The Essential Elements

*"Soil is primeval, and a living organism – we must
treasure it. At Highgrove, I have always practised
the art of feeding the soil rather than the plant."*

# 2  The Productive Gardens

*"I have striven for many years to explain to the visitor
about the food they eat – the way it is grown, its
processing and the end product. The centre of this activity
has always been the Walled Garden."*

# Introduction

## HRH The Prince of Wales

WHEN IT CAME TO GARDENING ORGANICALLY rather than conventionally at Highgrove, I think there were two crucial factors that persuaded me. The first was the fact that, when young, I had witnessed what seemed to me the wanton and unnecessary destruction of so much of this country's ancient, species-rich habitats and landscapes; whole field systems, thousands of miles of hedges, venerable woodlands, wildflower meadows – all those features which had developed over the centuries through the hand of man working in harmony with Nature – were ripped up in a mechanized instant in the name of what came to be known as "agri-industry". It was not the fault of farmers, of course – they were merely responding to what was being asked of them, or recommended to them by so-called experts, and Governments, at least at first, were responding to the food shortages during the Second World War. But whatever the motives, the consequences were dire: 186,000 miles of hedgerows, 95 per cent of wildflower meadows, 50 per cent of chalk grassland, 50 per cent of ancient lowland woodlands and 50 per cent of wetlands have been lost since 1945.

Although it may sound odd, before I had come to live at Highgrove I had begun to feel that this gigantic "experiment" with the whole of Nature, which increasingly seemed to me to be at risk of testing everything to destruction while at the same time extracting a cumulatively unsustainable harvest by artificial and progressively more toxic means, was both dangerous and short-sighted. I can only say that for some reason I felt "in my bones" that if you abuse Nature unnecessarily and fail to maintain a balance, then She will probably abuse you in return. This, of course, is "unscientific" because it depends on intuition rather than rational deduction. But, as we have since seen – with increasing alarm – by the time the deductive approach on its own has established the "evidence base", the whole delicate and intricately poised system has been tested to a point beyond which much, if anything, can be restored. So all this, along with a desire to put things back together again, was in the back of my mind when I arrived at Highgrove.

The second factor was when I turned to Lady Salisbury, and to her friend Dame Miriam Rothschild, for advice on how to tackle the garden and the process of habitat restoration. Both these remarkable ladies were formidable proponents of the organic approach and so, very quickly, I began to realize that there was an alternative and, I felt, a more balanced way of tending the earth and re-applying the time-honoured methods of husbandry that would ensure the long-term health of the soil. Through these two enthusiastic advisers I came to understand the fundamental principles of organic gardening and was able, gradually, to apply them at Highgrove. But I discovered that there is a great deal to learn and, furthermore, that one of the most essential sources of wisdom and practical knowledge lay in the books by Sir Albert Howard – probably the pre-eminent figure in the world of organic agriculture and horticulture – who, in turn, had learnt so much from ancient systems of cultivation during the forty years he spent working in India, where he held the office of Imperial Economic Botanist to the Government of India and then Agricultural Adviser to the states in Central India and Rajputana.

One of the great difficulties associated with the adoption of organic or, perhaps more appropriately, sustainable principles at the time I started turned out to be convincing others that you had not taken complete leave of your senses. With the massive growth in consumption of organic food today it might seem hard to imagine, but some twenty-five years ago it was virtually impossible to find anyone who had any knowledge of the management system required and who was happy to dispense with the ever-available chemical conveniences. Very quickly, I discovered that the essential rule for organic gardening is "take the rough with the smooth". I began, through observation, to realize that Nature doesn't allow you to have something for nothing, but nor does She inflict the same problems or diseases on your garden each year. People often ask me whether I was tempted to falter or was discouraged by the process of conversion. I can honestly say I wasn't, once I understood the value of patience and once I fully realized the need to put in as much as you take out from the soil. I think this is the most crucial lesson of all and once you appreciate that Nature is, in essence, a miraculous, living entity of Her own – above all striving to create a delicate balance at all times – you realize more fully how easily we can upset that balance if we treat this living entity as merely the sum of its component parts, to which we just happen, in a logical way, to have given chemical, biological or zoological descriptions.

In this sense, Nature does repay careful study and observation of Her minute details if organic gardening is to be successful. But it needs to be a study not wholly dependent on the laboratory investigation of each separate element, but on the intuitive appreciation of an underlying unity of all these seemingly separate elements that lies at the heart of the whole miraculous functioning of our Universe. One vital detail that increasingly became apparent to me was the need to maintain the health of the soil itself and of the extraordinary symbiotic relationship that exists between a vast host of bacteria, fungi and small invertebrates which, together with the all-important, but unseen, subterranean mychorrizal activity, make up the fundamental structure of the soil. Over thousands of years of hard-won experience, Mankind presumably discovered that Nature rewarded consideration towards the earth in terms of replacing the nutrients that had been taken out in the process of producing a crop. Hence, the long-held traditional practice of replacing lost nutrients through the application of manure or composted organic materials. In this way the health of the soil that has been thus nurtured is directly related to the health of what is produced from it and to its ability to fight off disease. The fundamental problem with an over-reliance on artificial fertilizers (apart from the fact that they are manufactured from a depleting oil-based derivative) and on chemical treatments for various pests and diseases is that they give nothing back to the soil and, ultimately, damage its intricate structure, thereby contributing to a loss of what might be called its inherent "immune system". If you consider that our own bodies are entirely organic and that when we finally die they revert to organic matter, or soil, then you begin to realize that what we do to ourselves – whether with an excess of antibiotic substances in our food or in our treatment – can be mirrored in what we do to the wider Nature from which we spring. Somehow we have succeeded in setting ourselves apart from the very essence of our being – Nature. Gradually, as you look further and deeper into the processes of Nature, you begin to realize that we ourselves are a microcosm of that vast, all-encompassing – essentially ordered – living entity. And the remarkable thing is that nothing is ever wasted. There is a constant process of renewing; of death followed by rebirth; of valuable materials being provided on a constantly sustaining basis, if managed with sympathy and continuity. Such is the case with the coppicing of certain tree species, like hazel or chestnut, or the pollarding of trees such as ash and oak and willow. [1]

Discovering through the organic approach that you can start to "close the loop" and create, as it were, a virtuous circle in terms of reducing unnecessary waste and pollution and, indeed, conserving water is enormously heartening. We have, I suppose, become so used to the advantage of convenience in so many aspects of life that we have failed to realize how much we have abused Nature in the process. To go on doing so regardless cannot conceivably be sustainable in the long-term. If we are looking for technological "fixes", then I happen to think they must be in *harmony* with the natural processes and, indeed, natural "laws" – for organic gardening *does* teach you that there are certain "laws" that need to be respected. The law of cause and effect is one of them. If we can reduce the causes – whether of pollution, waste, or whatever – then we will reduce the effect they produce on us, on our garden, on the wider environment and, ultimately, on the entire planet. All is interconnected and interwoven; but we seem to have lost sight of this essential truth and have become ever more separated from the inherent rhythms that lie at the heart of Nature. We have been dancing out of time with the music…

This is why it can become such a joy to learn again the excitement of seasonal things; to learn that it is possible – just – to find almost abandoned, traditional varieties of fruit and vegetables that are more resistant to the pests and diseases that assail the modern hybrids and which, therefore, fit naturally into an organic system without chemicals. Equally, it is a revelation to find that such old varieties have a quality and subtlety of taste that has been lost from our experience. As with the longed-for annual arrival of swallows, swifts and house-martins, looking forward to the imminent arrival of a particular fruit or vegetable at a particular time – and *only* for that precious time – becomes a treasured feature of one's existence and a rediscovery of what true culture is all about.

At Highgrove I have done my utmost to create a kind of archive of rare and endangered fruit, vegetables, trees and plants – a repository that, I hope, will help in a small way to preserve the essential biodiversity on which, ultimately, our survival depends. Too many of these ancient varieties, often developed over hundreds, if not thousands, of years, have been rashly discarded, or even prohibited by curious European legislation, and have only been kept in existence through the far-sightedness and determination of a very few organizations such as Garden Organic, which used to be known as The Henry Doubleday Research Association. Their work in this regard, together with the Elm Farm Research Centre and the Soil Association, cannot be over-emphasized in terms of its crucial importance for the future.

This book is designed to try and explain to those who may be interested in the organic approach, but perhaps hesitant and doubtful about taking the plunge for fear of all the complications, the various techniques and principles that need to be followed. In my previous book, *The Garden at Highgrove*, I couldn't help feeling that it lacked some of these more detailed explanations, and so this is an attempt to rectify that omission. Whatever the case, and whether your garden is large or small, I hope this book may just remind a few people of the urgent need to re-establish our connection with, and dependence upon, Nature and Her bounty. Our descendants are highly unlikely to thank us if it is ultimately found that we have indeed been guilty of treating Nature merely as a laboratory and not as a vast, integrated, living organism. Her bounty depends for its long-term continuity on the consideration and respect we show Her. "Stewardship" and "husbandry" may be considered old-fashioned words, but they encapsulate precisely that sense of *continuity of management* that is in harmony with the perpetual natural laws and rhythms of the Universe of which we are an integral part.

1 Coppicing – The regular removal of growth from woody plants at ground level to give a crop of useable material over a long period.
Pollarding – The regular removal of whole branches from established trees as a crop of timber leaving *in situ* the trunk and major branch stubs which then sprout and grow again to give crops of timber over a very long period.

# Prologue

*Stephanie Donaldson*

As we all become increasingly concerned about where our food comes from and what it contains, more and more of us are moving from being organic consumers to organic gardeners. We are discovering the pleasures and benefits of caring for the soil and nurturing plants to grow our own food.

You don't need a large piece of land or lots of equipment to be an organic gardener. What you do need is a desire to grow plants as naturally as possible, without recourse to artificial fertilizers or pesticides. Organic gardening used to be disparagingly referred to as "all muck and mystery", but thanks to the pioneering work of the Soil Association, Garden Organic and Prince Charles, there is an increasing understanding of the science, common sense and sustainability behind organic methods. The aim of this book is to share this knowledge.

The big difference between organic and conventional gardening is that the organic gardener's focus is on the soil, while the conventional gardener's focus is on the plant. It is an holistic system, which attends to the health of the entire ecosystem and not just the plant's needs. By the addition of compost, organic gardening creates and sustains a healthy soil full of nutrients and minerals that will naturally grow healthy plants. This is central to all organic gardening. Healthy plants are more able to resist pests and diseases and are nutritionally superior because they contain higher levels of essential vitamins and trace elements.

FIRST STEPS TO ORGANIC GARDENING

Know your soil – it is a living ecosystem. See pages 16–31 and page 158 for vital
    information about soil.

Choose the best possible location for a vegetable patch (ideally sunny and sheltered) and
    if there is nowhere suitable in your garden, consider getting an allotment.

Start with easy and rewarding vegetables – a single courgette plant can be very prolific as
    can a tepee of five runner beans.

You don't need to be growing food crops to garden organically.

Make compost – all kitchen and green waste can be recycled within the garden to add
    fertility and structure to the soil.

Collect rainwater – have as many water butts as you have downpipes. Rainwater is better
    for plants and is free.

Encourage wildlife by feeding the birds, providing habitats and growing plants to attract
    beneficial insects – they will help control pests.

Join GARDEN ORGANIC www.gardenorganic.org.uk (024 7630 3517) or the
    SOIL ASSOCIATION www.soilassociation.org (0117 314 5000) for expert help
    and information, and to support their work.

# The Highgrove Gardens
## A *bird's-eye view*

ONE OF THE MARKS of a fine garden is that it doesn't reveal all its charms at once and this is certainly the case at Highgrove. From the moment that visitors walk between the impressive pillars at the garden entrance, they are taken on a labyrinthine journey which leads from one delight to another.

Essentially the gardens divide into two areas: the first has the house at its heart, with a series of ornamental gardens, both formal and informal, to the South and West. These include the Cottage Garden, the Terrace Garden, the Thyme Walk, the Lily Pool Garden, the Sundial Garden and the Carpet Garden. The second area is centred on the productive Walled Garden, around which there are smaller productive gardens including the Model Fruit Garden and the Cutting Garden, as well as the Azalea Walk, the Southern Hemisphere Garden, the Woodland Garden and the Arboretum.

As visitors travel through the gardens, on pathways or the page, it is the Prince's wish that, while enjoying the beauty, they will reach the end of the journey with a deeper understanding and appreciation of the principles of organic gardening. These principles underlie everything that is done at Highgrove.

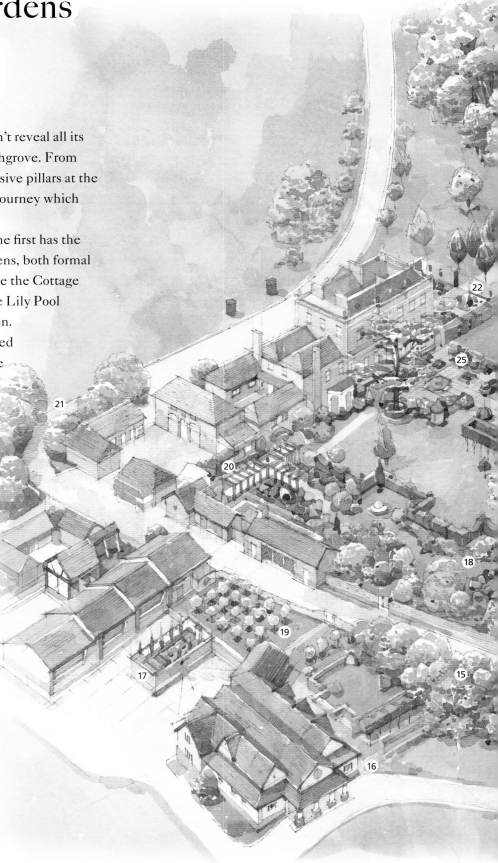

1. The Arboretum
2. Azalea Walk
3. Walled Garden
4. Orchard
5. New Orchard
6. Tree House
7. Wall of Gifts
8. Temple of Worthies
9. The Stumpery
10. Woodland Garden
11. Wildflower Meadow
12. Lily Pool Garden
13. Lime Avenue
14. The Dovecote
15. Old Carriage Wash
16. The Orchard Room
17. Carpet Garden
18. Cottage Garden
19. Lavender Orchard
20. Rose Pergola
21. Lime Avenue
22. Black and White/ Sundial Garden
23. The Sanctuary
24. Southern Hemisphere Garden
25. Terrace Garden
26. Thyme Walk

I

The Essential Elements

*"Soil is primeval, and a living organism – we must treasure it. At Highgrove, I have always practised the art of feeding the soil rather than the plant. This is done with the application of home-produced compost directly to the soil surface."*

HRH THE PRINCE OF WALES

# The soil

## *The raw material*

IT IS NO ACCIDENT that the leading organic organization in this country, of which the Prince of Wales is patron, is called the Soil Association. To organic farmers and gardeners, the soil is not merely a convenient medium in which to grow plants, but the very stuff of life itself. Consisting of ground-up rock, decayed organic matter, water and air, soil is seldom perceived or valued as a living thing, yet this mixture, teeming with microscopic organisms, supports all life on land. It is where the food-chain begins and ends.

In the natural world, soil fertility is successfully sustained without human intervention. The soil continuously renews itself through a process of recycling. As things die, they fall to the ground, decay and are broken down, naturally enriching the soil which in turn feeds the plants. Organic farmers and gardeners take that process and streamline it by making compost which will keep their land vital and productive. This is a core organic practice – nurturing and nourishing the soil to create conditions for growing healthy plants; plants that are stronger, more disease resistant and contain more vitamins and minerals than those grown in impoverished soil using artificial fertilizers and pesticides (see The Blueprint, page 158). A plant that has been grown by non-organic methods may look and even taste as good, but it will not contain the same levels of vitamins or as many trace elements as its organic equivalent.

Looked at in cross-section, soil divides into two layers – the topsoil, rich in nutrients and organic matter, and the subsoil which is largely devoid of either. The depth of topsoil varies enormously, ranging from inches to feet deep. The subsoil is often paler in colour and harder, if not impossible, to dig. Shallow soils can be improved over time by gradually breaking up the topmost layer of subsoil

*Prize-winning onions get the best possible start in Highgrove's home-made organic potting compost. This is a mixture of garden compost, sand, leaf mould and grit, formulated in specific proportions to suit the plants being grown.*

*Geological good fortune provided the deep and fertile soil in Highgrove's Walled Garden and 150 years of good husbandry has kept it that way. Even poor soils can become fertile and productive with the right care.*

and mixing it into the topsoil along with regular additions of compost. The main components of soil are rock and organic matter. Over millennia, rock has been ground down by the action of water and weather, resulting in soil particles of varying sizes and mineral content, depending on the geology of the area. Anything less than 2 millimetres in diameter is a soil particle. Sand has the largest particles and clay the smallest. Sand particles are the largest at 2–0.06 millimetres, silt particles measure from 0.06–0.002 millimetres, and anything below 0.02 millimetres in diameter is classified as clay.

The organic matter in soil comes from land-based living things. Every living thing, animal or vegetable, eventually dies, decays and returns to the soil. In so doing, it contributes nutrients and humus, which create a fertile mixture when combined with the soil particles. Humus is the well-decayed organic matter that gives the soil its structure and aids aeration and moisture retention. Soil structure is defined as the way that the particles are held together. This relates to the humus content, electrical conductivity and animal life in the soil. For example,

THE ELEMENTS OF ORGANIC GARDENING

*Not long ago the Cutting Garden – a remnant of an earlier nursery – was an area of ground infested with bindweed and ground elder. Seven years of double digging, combined with mulching, has cleared the weeds and allowed an easily maintained garden to be established.*

*In the Walled Garden, the rich soil allows many of the beds to produce two crops a year as well as catch crops, such as lettuce and spinach, which do not need to be included in the rotation plans.*

a healthy worm population is a good sign. Worms feed on and process decaying organic matter and are most prolific in soils that are rich in this substance.

Technically, humus is classified as a colloid, which means it has the ability to hold on to nutrients through electrostatic charges. Humus colloids tend to have a negative charge and this enables them to attract the largely positively charged nutrients which will readily adhere to them. Once an organic gardener understands why a good humus content is essential in the soil (to hold on to the nutrients that make it fertile) soil management becomes much easier. This emphasis on the importance of humus in the soil is the defining difference between organic and non-organic gardening and farming.

Healthy, fertile soils are rich in microbiological life in the form of bacteria, fungi, and macro- and micro-fauna such as earthworms, beetles and nematodes (microscopic roundworms). The more organic matter there is in the soil the wider the range of microbes. These diverse micro-organisms transform organic matter into nutrients, hormones and vitamins which can be absorbed by plants. In association with leguminous plants (peas and beans), they also have the ability to transfer nitrogen from the air to the soil.

Of the many types of bacteria in the soil, many are beneficial, others less so. They feed by secreting enzymes which dissolve their surroundings into a digestible form. They speed up the process of decomposition and feed on many harmful substances, rendering them harmless. Mycorrhizal fungi live on the roots of plants, aid water retention in the root area and also make nutrients available. These occur naturally in a healthy soil and their presence is boosted by the regular addition of compost.

In recent years gardeners have been able to buy products that contain myccorhiza in the form of "effective micro-organisms" or mycorrhizal dips. These may help short-term, but if myccorhiza are not naturally present in the soil they will soon die off.

## Soil types

Understanding the type of soil in a garden is an essential part of growing plants successfully. At its simplest it requires nothing more than bending down, picking up a small quantity of soil and rubbing it between thumb and forefinger. If it is light in weight, feels coarse and runs through your fingers, it is predominantly sand; if it is heavy, feels smooth, readily sticks together and smears on the skin it is a clay soil. Of course, there are many points in between, and somewhere midway between the two extremes there is silt, which is more generally known as loam when it combines with organic matter, sand and clay. A soil's texture is defined by the proportion of sand, silt and clay it contains.

*Dennis Brown stands in the middle of a bed of his prize-winning onions. At the end of his working day in the Walled Garden he goes next door to tend the onions in his own garden.*

*The deep, rich, friable soil in the Walled Garden is ideal for growing prolific crops of potatoes. As potatoes are among Prince Charles's favourite vegetables, several varieties are grown, including 'Arran Pilot', 'Desiree' and 'Pink Fir Apple'.*

Sandy soils consist of coarse particles. This means that there are plenty of air spaces between the grains of sand, making it very free draining and consequently poor at retaining moisture. It is known as a hungry soil because nutrients are easily washed out during rain or watering. On the plus side, it warms up early in the year, is always is easy to dig and can be fertile and productive provided that it is regularly enriched with compost. No garden soil is pure sand, but if it is more sand than loam it is known as loamy sand, while if loam predominates it is a sandy loam.

Silt is the midpoint between sand and clay with particles that are not as large as sand or as small as clay. It is generally formed as sediment in lake beds and river floodplains. The most fertile and workable soils usually contain silt which, when combined with clay, sand and organic matter, creates loam. There are different classifications of loam depending on the amount of sand or clay that is present. These range from silt-loam, where very little sand or clay is present, to clay-loam which is an equal mix of sand, silt and clay.

Clay has the smallest soil particles, so small that they can be suspended in water. Because they are so fine they adhere together readily, making a solid mass and excluding air, which means that they easily become waterlogged. Another problem with clay soils is that they can be difficult to cultivate for much of the year. In Winter they are cold, very wet and heavy, and any attempt to cultivate risks doing further damage to the structure; in Summer they bake hard. However, clay soils do retain nutrients and if the texture is improved by regular additions of compost and grit, they will prove very fertile.

There is a simple way to test the ratio of different particles in your soil and obtain a visual confirmation of its composition. Half-fill a lidded glass container (a tall, narrow jar is ideal) with soil, then add water until the jar is three-quarters full. Replace the lid and shake the jar vigorously for a minute or two, until all the particles are suspended in the water. Store in a dark place to avoid algae turning the water green and leave it for a couple of days, possibly longer for heavy soil as the finest clay particles can be slow to settle. Gradually, during this time, by a process known as Brownian Movement, the particles will settle in stratified layers. The largest particles (sand) will go to the bottom and the finest (clay) to the top. The organic matter generally floats on the surface. By measuring the total height of all the layers in the jar and then the individual layers (except the water), you can calculate the proportion of sand, silt, clay and organic matter in your soil.

In addition to the three main types of soil – sand, silt and clay – there are two more that don't fit neatly into these categories and cannot be defined by particle size. These are peat soils, and chalk and limestone soils.

Peat soils consist of partially decomposed vegetation which decayed underwater in swamps and bogs. The peat bog is a classic example of anaerobic (without air) decomposition. In this watery environment the nitrogen-loving bacteria break down vegetation, leaving humus that is high in organic matter, but virtually depleted of nitrogen. It has accumulated over thousands of years and as the water receded it left a crumbly, water-retentive material. Although low in nutrients it can readily be enriched with compost, is easy to work and will grow superb crops. This quality has led to the over-extraction of peat for commercial horticulture and it has now become an endangered resource.

Chalk and limestone soils are often poor and shallow so can be difficult to cultivate. Although they contain soil particles, they are predominantly chalk or limestone which limits the plants that can be grown. Improving this soil is a long, hard process and the usual response to someone who asks what they can do about the chalky soil in their garden is, "Move".

A soil's pH is the measurement of its acidity or alkalinity and is determined by the amount of lime it contains. It affects the availability of all nutrients, so it is vital that it is understood by gardeners. Soil test kits are useful for determining whether a soil is acid, neutral or alkaline, but cannot always be relied upon to give more accurate readings. The pH level is measured on a scale of 1 to 14. Below 7 is acid, above 7 is alkaline, while the region of 6.6 to 7.3 is usually considered neutral. The pH of good compost is usually on the slightly acid side of neutral.

Weeds that are indigenous to your area and the plants that do well in the garden can be indicators of soil pH. Sorrel, plantain and knotgrass grow in acid soils, while poppies and charlock prefer alkaline conditions. Nettles, chickweed and groundsel are all common weeds in well-balanced fertile soil.

The soil types in the garden at Highgrove provide an interesting challenge to the gardening staff and, at the same time, diversity within the garden. Highgrove soil is very variable. Some is deep, fertile loam, while other parts consist of poor, shallow soil. Much consists of 18 inches of loam over blue lias clay, which is soft and dark-coloured and is of the type found in the fossil-rich cliffs at Lyme Regis in Dorset. Faced with a large heap of the soil when a soakaway was dug in the field below the Orchard Room, Prince Charles realized that this was a problem that could have a useful outcome – the soil was ideal for making cob bricks. Cob, a traditional, and very environmentally friendly building material, is a mixture of clay, sharp sand, chopped straw and crushed limestone. Fifteen hundred cob bricks were made by ramming the mixture into wooden moulds and baking them in the sun. The process wasn't always easy because when the bricks got wet they dissolved into a muddy mess, but they had simply to be reformed and started again. The cob bricks were subsequently used to build The Sanctuary in the Arboretum. Once complete, the building was made waterproof by rendering it with a cob mix to which a small amount of Portland cement had been added.

In some other parts of Highgrove the soil is Cotswold brash, a thin, stony, poor soil 4–6 inches deep over a limestone base. The worst area on the estate is the site of the Wildflower Meadow where the shallow impoverished condition is a positive benefit. Fertility is the enemy of the wild flower.

*The lush foliage and abundant flowers growing in front of The Temple of Worthies, with its relief of Queen Elizabeth The Queen Mother, in the Woodland Garden are evidence of the fertility of the soil that lies beneath.*

The Wildflower Meadow is managed in such a way as to keep fertility low by haymaking and grazing. If soil is very fertile, too much grass will grow at the expense of flowers.

Suffolk Punch horses are used to cut and cart some of the hay from the Wildflower Meadow. It is important to remove the hay each year; if it is left to rot down it will increase the meadow's fertility.

The final soil type within the garden is forest marble. This soil is as good as it gets – 4 feet 6 inches of sandy acid loam over limestone with a pH of 6.5. It is very unusual and one of its many useful qualities is that rhododendrons can be grown in open ground in an area where the presence of lime in the soil would usually make this impossible.

Two million years ago this corner of Gloucestershire was a lagoon and as the water receded it left behind this fine fertile legacy. It is a soil type that Highgrove shares with the National Arboretum at Westonbirt and it also runs through nearby Tetbury and Highgrove's Home Farm, which is on the other side of town. At Home Farm, the vegetables for their organic box scheme are grown on this soil. Almost two centuries ago, forest marble was also recognized as something special by the people who laid out the productive gardens at Highgrove and its presence influenced the location of the Walled Garden. Now, with the addition of 150 years of compost, they have what the gardeners call "black gold".

However, even if your own garden lacks these particular advantages, there is much that can be done to enhance the soil and prepare it for planting. It is essential to familiarize yourself with the soil by handling it. We have become frightened to do so, thinking of earth as dirty and unhealthy, yet plunging your hands into rich friable soil is a wonderful experience. It feels good to the touch

*Gardener Dennis Brown prepares the deep, rich loam in the Walled Garden for planting. Where appropriate, manure is added and rotavated in, and the ground is raked to form a fine tilth.*

and "earths" you in the most literal of senses. It smells good too, especially after a shower of rain on a warm Summer's day. A soil that smells sour or unpleasant indicates poor aeration or drainage, or pollution, and should be handled with care. But as Paul Alexander, senior soil scientist at RHS Wisley, says, "I think there is no such thing as a problem soil – just soil that needs more work and thought."

Poor soil, from heavy clay to light sand, can have its structure and fertility improved by growing green manures and regularly adding compost or well-rotted farmyard manure. The gardens of newly built houses can prove to be a particular challenge. Too often the topsoil has been stripped off and the subsoil compacted, then covered with turf to disguise what lies beneath. In this instance it is essential to introduce and incorporate large quantities of organic matter in the form of farmyard manure, spent hops, garden compost, soil conditioner, mushroom compost or peat substitutes. Gradually, with each addition, the soil will improve.

The aim of all soil improvement is to produce a soil that invites you to touch it; if it looks cold, clammy and lumpy, or thin and dry you won't enjoy handling it, and, more importantly, seeds and young plants won't like it either. They may survive, but are less likely to thrive.

## Feeding the soil

Highgrove uses two methods of composting – aerobic (with air) and anaerobic (without air). They have different purposes. Aerobic decomposition, using garden and stable waste, produces a compost rich in nitrogen that feeds the soil and the plants that grow in it. Anaerobic decomposition, using fallen leaves, produces a mould (as in leaf mould) which is high in humus but low in nitrogen. This is used to improve soil structure and is also a component of the Highgrove potting mixtures. It is called "mould" because this relates to the fungi that are involved in the rotting process

These two methods employ different bacteria. Aerobic composting uses oxygen-loving bacteria, while anaerobic composting uses those that are nitrogen loving. When the right conditions are created for oxygen-loving bacteria , none of the nitrogen-loving bacteria become involved. This results in the nitrogen being retained through the composting process to be used by plants.

There are four main rules for successful aerobic composting. Use the correct raw materials to nurture the aerobic bacteria. Balance the carbon/nitrogen ratio 50:50. Exclude leaves and woody material. Turn the heap as frequently as possible. At Highgrove the heaps are turned once a week, moving the compost from one bin to another. This is the ideal way to make compost because it causes the aerobic bacteria to multiply and speeds up the process. Heat is produced as a by-product and kills off pathogens, fungi and weed seeds. By turning regularly,

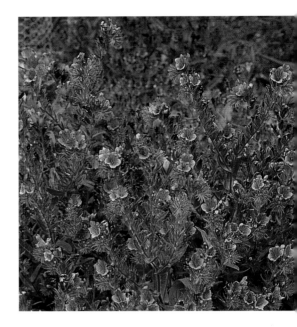

*Green manures are sown after a crop has been harvested and dug in shortly before planting a new crop. Traditionally, leguminous crops are used, but beneficial insect-attracting plants such as* Echium *'Blue Bedder' are also suitable.*

*"My philosophy of compost is that it is everything the garden needs because it is made out of everything from the garden."*

HEAD GARDENER DAVID HOWARD

the raw material is transformed into compost in 12 to 16 weeks. The speed relates directly to the turning; it is possible to make compost in four to six weeks if you turn it often enough.

This may all sound frighteningly labour intensive to gardeners who have neither the time nor the equipment (at Highgrove they use a small tractor), but commercially produced rotating compost bins are an effective solution for busy people. Positioned next to the garden path and given a spin daily as you walk past, the result will be the finest possible compost in the shortest period of time.

All compost heaps must be managed; if they are left to their own devices the nutrients (and the value) of the compost will be depleted. But if, despite your best intentions, the compost heap remains unturned, the compost will still be a wonderful soil conditioner, although it will have fewer nutrients and it will be necessary to add an organic fertilizer, such as fish, blood and bone.

Making compost at Highgrove is not just about how it is managed, it is also about what goes into it. The mix is an equal amount of carbon and nitrogen – straw and grass clippings. On its own, straw will take a year to decompose because it consists of 90 per cent carbon, while grass is 90 per cent nitrogen and water and will decompose very quickly. Grass is so moist that it quickly clumps together and goes anaerobic if the air cannot get to it. The first sign of this is the smell of ammonia, a by-product of anaerobic decomposition.

*At Highgrove they make a highly nutritious compost in 12 weeks by carefully balancing the ingredients and turning the compost heaps weekly. Once composting is complete, it is moved undercover to prevent nutrients leaching out.*

*Steam rising from the compost is evidence of the enormous heat that is generated by aerobic bacteria as they digest the organic matter and transform it into compost.*

By mixing straw and grass together, the ideal conditions are created for aerobic composting to take place. Gardeners can buy in straw for their own compost heaps. The Highgrove straw is mainly farm stable waste, although chicken and pigeon manure are also added from time to time; the best way to process this animal waste is by composting it. During the Summer months, nitrogen-rich kitchen and florist's waste and dead-headed flowers are also added, along with the grass clippings. Theoretically, invasive perennial weeds such as docks, thistles, bindweed and ground elder are thoroughly dried before being added to the heap, but currently they are helping to fill a large hole on the farm prior to landscaping.

No Autumn leaves or woody material are put into the compost heap. This is because cellulose, lignin and tannin are all complex carbon compounds which take a long time to break down; a felled tree can take a hundred years to decompose. Although shredding leaves or wood does speed things up, adding leaves or wood in any form lengthens the composting process.

The Highgrove compost bins are purpose-made. The back and side walls are made from a double layer of alternating planks stuffed with straw; a cheap and effective way of providing insulation while allowing air circulation. "You don't need to copy this," says head gardener David Howard. "Devise something suitable for your garden, but preferably not on a solid base as this prevents worms migrating into the compost from the soil below. You can make similar bins out of recycled wooden pallets. They don't need to be big, but there do need to be three bays, so that you can keep turning the compost from one bay to another." The bins are only covered during the Winter months to prevent rain washing out the nutrients.

Once the compost is made it is stored under cover in the open barn. Protecting it in this way is essential or the nitrogen (which has a weak electrical charge that is easily removed by water) will leach out. Home-made compost is best stored in black plastic sacks or a bin.

The finished compost is spread as a thin mulch (up to an inch) on the surface of beds and borders. The reason that it is such a thin layer is that the aim is only to return what has been removed; deep mulches rarely occur in the natural world. Compost is spread in early Spring so that the nutrients aren't leached out during the Winter months and are available when the plants need them most. It is not incorporated because the worms will do this and make a better job of it. The role of the compost is not weed suppression but to feed the soil for the forthcoming season. Some compost is held back for the potting mixtures where it makes up a quarter of the bulk (see The Blueprint, page 158 for the recipe).

Anaerobic composting is used in the Highgrove gardens to recycle the huge quantities of fallen leaves by turning them into leaf mould. This is used as a valuable soil conditioner and an ingredient in the potting mixes. Anaerobic composting involves creating the right conditions for nitrogen-loving bacteria (think peat bog). The leaves are stacked in a clamp (heap) in a woodland copse, and as they settle the oxygen is progressively excluded, allowing the nitrogen-loving bacteria to get to work breaking down the tannins and lignins in the leaves. By exposing them to the elements in a deep layer that is undisturbed for at least two years, the nitrifying bacteria transform the leaves into fine organic matter that is high in humus and low in nitrogen. This process is aided by naturally occurring myccorhizal fungi which assist in the decomposition.

*Once a year a thin layer of compost is spread on all the beds in the ornamental gardens. The aim is to replace the nutrients that have been used by the plants rather than to mulch the soil. Earthworms will incorporate it into the soil.*

As a peat substitute, well-made leaf mould is virtually indistinguishable in seed and potting mixes and it is also a wonderful soil conditioner, although it has virtually no food value. In smaller gardens, the simplest way to make leaf mould is to stack fallen leaves in a bin made from four fence posts surrounded by wire netting. Compact the leaves as much as possible to create the right conditions for the nitrogen-loving bacteria to get to work; this will also allow you to keep adding leaves as they fall.

The leaf mould is used in the making of Highgrove's potting and seed mediums. Based entirely on natural materials, they are a mix of equal parts of leaf mould, garden compost, unsterilized loam and sharp sand. The loam isn't sterilized because this would involve killing the good as well as the bad bacteria. This does introduce some weed seeds, but the Highgrove gardeners take a philosophical view of weeding, saying, "That's what gardeners do." Everything in the mix originates on the estate with the exception of the sharp sand, but as it is a relatively inert product, Highgrove is happy to import this essential ingredient.

To make a natural growing medium, sand is needed for drainage, compost for food, leaf mould for humus, and unsterilized loam for beneficial bacteria and myccorhiza. Because humus is a negatively charged colloid (in simple terms "gluey"), nutrients adhere to it, so the greater the humus content the greater the ability of the medium to contain nutrients. This is why the commercial horticultural industry is so attached to using peat – it is one huge colloid for holding on to the artificial fertilizers.

The aim is to create a perfect medium for plants to grow in. The sharp sand is added because pots are an artificial environment and it is necessary to improve drainage. The medium consists of roughly equal parts of the four ingredients, but this is variable. For example, ferns prefer less sand and more leaf mould, while cacti (if they were grown at Highgrove) would require more sand and less leaf mould. The recipe is not set in stone and, unlike bought-in composts, allows mixes to be individually tailored to suit the plants. Peat-free composts are often criticized for a lack of consistency, but at Highgrove the germination and growth rates compare well with commercial composts. This was confirmed when Wisley soil scientist Paul Alexander did an analysis that showed very favourable results. Plants that stay in pots for three to six months need no extra organic fertilizer, but for long-term container planting, the slow-release natural fertilizer, fish, blood and bone, is added to the medium.

The possibilities of large-scale worm composting at Highgrove are also currently under consideration. The initiative for this came from Rosie Bowyer, a student from Writtle College who recently spent a training year working in the Highgrove gardens. She is writing her dissertation on the use of worm compost in potting mixes. If all goes well, vermiculture will be included in the composting regime and it will become a component of the Highgrove mixes.

*The Bocking 14 strain of comfrey is used to make the organic liquid feed that is used at Highgrove. The comfrey is cut and soaked in water to create a highly nutritious but very smelly brew.*

*The vigorous health of the plants in Highgrove's greenhouses is a credit to the quality of the home-produced potting mixtures and the organic growing methods. During Spring and Summer, plants are given a regular liquid feed of the comfrey brew.*

Any liquid feeds and plant tonics used at Highgrove are all natural. As David Howard says, "When using natural feeds there is a huge buffering effect which means it is hard to overdose when applying them."

Liquid feed is primarily used in the glasshouses, the nursery and for permanently potted plants. Jess Usher is the Highgrove specialist. She mixes up regular batches of a comfrey brew using a variety called Bocking 14. Plants are available from the organic gardening charity HDRA (now renamed Garden Organic). The Bocking 14 variety is superior to other types of comfrey because it is fast growing, very high in nutrients and does not set seed or have a creeping root, so it will not colonize the garden. Once the comfrey is established, the leaves can be cut three or four times a year with early Autumn, at the latest, being the time for the final cut. A Spring mulch of compost is all that is needed to keep the plants productive.

Liquid comfrey is made by steeping the cut leaves in a tub of water. As the leaves rot down, rather like a stock pot, more leaves are added. The result is an extremely smelly, putrid brew that is not for the faint-hearted. However, it is rich in nitrogen and phosphorus and particularly high in potash, so makes a very valuable liquid feed. From the first cut, the comfrey liquid is generally useable in two weeks and is applied at a roughly 10 per cent dilution, or more simply a jam jar full to a 1-gallon can of water.

When necessary, calcified seaweed (obtained from a Soil Association certificated source) is used as a tonic for plants that are failing. In the Walled Garden it is being applied to the box hedging to help the plants recover from an attack of box blight.

# Water

WITHOUT WATER NOTHING will grow. From microscopic soil organisms to the mightiest oak tree, everything is reliant on water to stay alive. While soil is fundamental, it cannot exist without water and, with water, comes life: for the soil, for the plants that grow in it and for the animals eating those plants. Already, the simplest of food chains has started and it is easy to see how essential water is to this process.

As gardeners, in the recent past we have been profligate with water, confident that it would replenish itself. After all, the British Isles are renowned for their greenness and for the frequency of rain, and in dry weather turning on the tap to give the garden a good soak couldn't be easier. In some gardens, even turning on the tap has become obsolete as timers, and automatic irrigation systems have taken over the task of watering.

But now, through a combination of overuse and climate change, the most populated areas of the country are running out of water. We must learn to be more self-reliant by harvesting and conserving water, and by being more intelligent about how we use it.

There are few natural water courses on the Highgrove Estate. Among these are the evocatively named "winterbournes". These small ephemeral streams only flow from November to April (or even less in a dry Winter), which means that they are of no practical use as a source of water for the gardens. As a result, the use of water at Highgrove relies primarily on conservation. It is saved in three ways: rainwater, water recycled from sewage through the reed-bed water-purification system, and groundwater from a borehole.

The simplest method of rainwater harvesting at Highgrove is a downpipe leading into a water butt or into the old slate water tanks in the greenhouses, something any gardener can do. But large-scale rainwater harvesting is also

*Virtually all the water used at Highgrove, both for water features and for watering plants, is recycled through the reed-bed sewage system or harvested from the roofs of the various buildings. It is then stored underground, before being pumped to where it is needed.*

> *"In my early days at Highgrove I began to realize that water conservation was going to be paramount in the development of the garden: the reed-bed sewage system, the rainwater tank, the borehole, the composted woodchip mulches and the old carpet were all going to play their part."*

HRH THE PRINCE OF WALES

employed. The harvesting system uses a huge 23,000-gallon underground holding tank that collects the rain from the roofs of the house, the Orchard Room and the beef buildings. This system has an historical precedent. Before the arrival of mains water at Highgrove, the estate used an underground water storage tank and it was this that inspired Prince Charles to set up a similar system. The subterranean reservoir ensures there is enough water available to allow the gardeners to operate a fairly simple irrigation system that moves water to where it is needed, using, as appropriate, a combination of "leaky pipes", sprinklers or watering points.

This can be done on a smaller scale in most gardens. A water butt positioned at a downpipe is the beginning of rainwater harvesting and when the butt is fitted with an overflow pipe, the excess water can be fed into a larger holding tank. A search on the internet using the subject "rainwater harvesting" or "rainwater tanks" provides a number of suppliers of both underground and overground tanks, including recycled fruit juice containers that hold 330 gallons of water – about seven times that of the average water butt. It is also possible to have a professionally designed system installed that will make use of all the grey water from the house, as well as collecting rainwater. The Department of the Environment offers impartial advice about this on its website.

Conserving water at Highgrove is as much about recycling as it is about harvesting, and the reed-bed sewage system is central to this. A huge inverted concrete chamber below ground acts as the receptor tank for all the waste from the estate dwellings and the Orchard Room. When the tank is one-third full, pumps cut in (because the land is flat the whole system is maintained by electric pumps) and move the waste into one of three bark-filled pits (more inverted concrete chambers). These pits are five-sixths filled with coarse-grade bark and as the effluent drains through, the solids and liquids are separated and the effluent goes back to a smaller tank. When this, in turn, is one-third full, the water is removed automatically and pumped into the reed bed. The reed bed is a rectangle measuring 12 by 30 feet, surrounded by a wall of 4 feet 6 inches. It is filled with layered aggregate, starting with boulders at the bottom and getting progressively smaller, with sand on the surface. The sand is planted with Norfolk reed.

*Water purified by the reed-bed sewage system eventually enters this pond, from where it is pumped into the storage tank or discharged into a ditch that leads to a river. In 17 years of testing no pollutants have been found in this water.*

Water from the small tank is pumped into the top of the reed bed and allowed to flood the surface. Two cleaning processes then take place, filtration (which removes suspended solids) and (as part of its natural growing process) the reed removes the soluble nitrates and phosphates from the water and uses them as plant food. The water then percolates through the aggregates, out at the bottom of the wall through drainage holes and into the willow bed planted in the adjoining open ground.

Here the same two processes are repeated: the water filters through the soil removing any residual solids, and the willow takes any remaining nitrates and phosphates out of the water.

The rich supply of plant nutrients stimulates the reeds and the willows to put on a remarkable 7–8 feet of growth annually, so both must be coppiced in January to keep them under control. Ideally, the reeds would be harvested for thatching, but the area of the reed bed is not large enough to produce a viable quantity, so they are chipped instead. The gardeners take all the willow they need for plant supports and the remainder is used by two basket makers who weave it into items that are sold in the shop.

*The reeds and willow put on prodigious growth, growing more than 7 feet a year as they feed on the nutrients in the water. They are cut and harvested each January to keep them under control. The reeds are chipped and the willow is used for plant supports and basket making.*

Once the water has filtered through the willow bed, it gathers in another collecting tank and is pumped into the flowform (see The Blueprint, page 159), which aerates and energizes the water, before it flows over a cascade and enters the pond. The water, now pure, is discharged from the pond into a drain that leads to an open ditch. This enters a river two miles South of Tetbury. The efficiency of the reed-bed system ensures that no pollutants enter the river system. It is tested four times a year by the Environment Agency and in 17 years of testing there has never been an adverse result.

The reed-bed sewage system and rainwater harvesting were built as separate units. Now that they have been integrated, the gardeners can draw water from

either the holding tank or the pond for use in the irrigation system. Pioneers often find that early developments, like these two systems, need updating and it is only at a later stage that efficiencies become apparent. The idea of linking the two systems occurred as a result of a very dry Summer when the water from the pond kept evaporating before it could be used.

The third method of water conservation, the borehole behind the Orchard Room, is used only as a last resort. In the eight years that David Howard has been head gardener, he can count on the fingers of one hand the number of times it has been drawn from, but it is a reassuring back-up if other water sources run low.

Water is always used carefully at Highgrove. Overwhelmingly, the gardens rely on the irrigation system, using stored or recycled water. The lawns are never watered; if they go brown in Summer they will soon recover once it has rained. In the event of a drought there is a hierarchy of need, with pots at the head of the queue, then the productive gardens and finally the ornamental borders.

Because watering is labour intensive, everything is grown hard, encouraging the plants to root deeply and find their own moisture. As explained earlier in the section on compost (see page 29), compost is used primarily as a feed rather than a mulch on the beds and borders, but its moisture-retaining qualities are useful too. In the Walled Garden, where the soil is deep, moist and fertile, the beds don't need to be mulched at all. Although seemingly going against the common advice to organic gardeners to mulch deeply, the only plants that are lost at Highgrove in hot, dry weather are newly planted trees. Where specific plants have specific needs, such as moisture and shelter, a place is found within the garden that will provide these. For example, in the case of tender exotics, this is beneath the tree canopy in the Arboretum where the moist shade provides ideal conditions for raising these plants.

*The moss-covered fountain at the centre of the dipping pool in the Walled Garden is a popular drinking and bathing place for the wild birds, which are invaluable as pest controllers.*

## Ponds and pools

The addition of a pond, however small, is one of the most valuable wildlife assets in any garden, especially if it is an informal pond with gently sloping banks where birds and animals can drink and marginal plants provide shelter. At Highgrove, the Carriage Wash is just such a place. In the 19th century, carriages were driven through shallow ponds like this to remove accumulated mud from the roads before going into the stable yard. It had been filled in before Prince Charles's arrival and was practically invisible, but he had it re-excavated and planted with flag iris, rushes and other marginal plants. Now it is a natural pool fed by rainwater and is largely left alone as a favourite haunt of amphibians and birds.

With the exception of the old dewpond in outlying woodland, the other ponds and pools at Highgrove are probably better described as water features. There is the Terrace Pool in front of the West facade of the house, the Lily Pool at the end of the Thyme Walk, the Woodland Garden Pool, and the Dipping Pool in the Walled Garden.

Maintenance of the ornamental ponds and pools is minimal. The moving water seems to keep duckweed and blanket weed at bay, but if a problem does develop, the pond is emptied out and scrubbed clean before it is refilled. In general, the ponds without fish are more problem-prone, while those with fish are easier to control. The fish, mainly rudd, arrived unbidden, presumably as eggs on the feet of birds. They have done so well that the population has twice had to be reduced and fish re-homed. The three species of dragonfly that hover on their margins, and the regular visits by mallard ducks, moorhens and heron, are proof of how attractive these ponds and pools are to wildlife.

*The rainwater-fed Carriage Wash pond is left largely to its own devices so that amphibians and birds can breed undisturbed. Its gently sloping banks, planted with marginal plants, make a perfect habitat for wildlife.*

*The Woodland Garden pool is also attractive to local wildlife. The island in the centre of the pond has been constructed from redundant stone and is topped by a flamboyant "hat" of gunnera.*

2

The Productive Gardens

*"I have striven for many years to explain to the visitors about the food they eat – the way it is grown, its processing and the end product. The centre of this activity has always been the Walled Garden, whether it is the way Dennis Brown manages his cabbages and cauliflowers or the display that he creates each year to emphasize the importance of heritage seed varieties."*

HRH THE PRINCE OF WALES

# The Walled Garden

THE WALLED GARDEN, with its harmonious blend of beauty and utility, is one of Prince Charles's favourite places and it is easy to understand why. It is far more than a sheltered growing area; the sense of enclosure evokes an emotional response, a feeling of safety and privacy, alongside its practical purpose as a kitchen garden.

For the organic gardener, sensitivity to one's surroundings and a feeling of connection with a place are both aspects of caring for the soil and the environment. The focus is on stewardship rather than ownership, with the garden and the soil nurtured in such a way that productivity is maintained while taking care to keep fertility intact for future generations.

When Prince Charles arrived at Highgrove, the Walled Garden was derelict; its walls were in a state of disrepair with large sections missing and the whole area was infested with perennial weeds. Prior to this, the garden had supplied Highgrove with its fruit and vegetables for well over a hundred years. With its deep, rich, forest marble soil it was too good to be used for less productive purposes, so its walls were repaired, everything was grubbed out, beds were made and new paths were laid.

Just under one acre in extent, the Walled Garden is a productive kitchen garden, but an ornamental one too due to its strong symmetrical design. This design was the work of Prince Charles and his gardening mentor Lady Salisbury. The garden is divided into four quarters separated by wide gravel paths and each quarter is further divided into four squares or triangles, edged with box hedging. Although not apparent from the ground, an aerial view reveals that these beds are representations of the flags of St George and St Andrew. Prince Charles explains, "I had to simplify the original design because it was becoming too ambitious and I thought the Crosses would be appropriate and make the box hedges easier to

*The design of the Walled Garden beds is decorative, but care has been taken to make sure that they are practical too. This is a highly productive area of the garden which must earn its keep in vegetables for the kitchen.*

*The wide paths make access and maintenance easy. Narrow paths are a false economy as they make it difficult to keep a garden tidy. Ideally, a path should be wide enough to move a wheelbarrow along it without causing any damage.*

maintain." At the centre of each flag there is an arbour over which are trained Paul's Himalayan Musk roses, honeysuckle, clematis and wisteria.

At the very centre of the garden is the original dipping pool, more recently made into a water feature. Its fountain is heavy with moss and drips constantly, attracting birds to drink and bathe in its tiered bowls. Radiating out from the pool are four curved culinary herb beds set into the gravel paths with a rosemary hedge as a backdrop. Each May the rosemary is cut back and the clippings are used to make rosemary oil for the shop. Encircling the rosemary hedge is a crown formed from 20 trained *Malus* 'Golden Hornet', an ornamental crab apple which acts as a decorative pollinator. These trees have proved a mixed blessing, however; the festoon design is not the best growing shape and the dense foliage harbours pests and diseases. In an attempt to rectify this, the trees have been radically pruned to open their centres and remove the mat of growth on top. Their future shape is still uncertain, depending on how well they recover from surgery.

All the beds and borders are brick-edged, with grass or brick paths leading between the low box hedges to the central arbours. The beds are sufficiently large in area to ensure that they are easy to work and will grow a substantial crop.

LEFT: *Apple trees, which have been trained over a metal framework of arches, enclose the main path in the garden. Not only is this highly decorative, especially when they are in blossom, but it also turns the path into a productive space.*

ABOVE: *Sweet peas are trained over arches made from hazel and willow harvested on the estate. They form a fragrant tunnel over the diagonal paths.*

An earlier, far more intricate design for the kitchen garden was abandoned when Prince Charles realized that it would be hugely labour intensive to maintain and not nearly as productive.

This is an important consideration for anyone designing a kitchen garden. Paths need to be wide to allow easy access and beds large enough to grow all the vegetables you want. If space is limited, it is better to have fewer, larger beds than many small ones. This may limit the number of varieties that can be grown, but it is better than trying to grow small quantities of many different vegetables. Aim to produce sufficient quantities for at least five meals from any single variety, or you will not be repaid for the effort you have put into growing the plants.

## Glasshouse crops

Traditionally, the Productive Gardens on an estate supply the house with everything it needs in the way of fruit, vegetables and flowers. At Highgrove, they also play a vital role in supplying most of the produce and flowers for the busy round of fund-raising events and receptions which take place in the Orchard Room in aid of The Prince's Trust and other charitable causes.

Highgrove's productive gardens are given an early start in the greenhouses and cold frames. By the time Dennis Brown begins direct-sowing seeds in the Walled Garden, there are already pickable crops of carrots, spinach, basil and self-blanching celery in the cold frames. The frames are invaluable for this purpose; oriented to the South, they make the very best of the sun and shelter the plants from chill winds and frost. On warm days the lights (the glazed lids) are propped open to allow ventilation, but they can be left shut in cold weather.

The frames are also used to harden-off plants that have been raised in the greenhouses and need gradual exposure to cooler temperatures before they can be planted out in the Walled Garden. Hardening-off usually takes about a week and ensures that plants are not shocked by a sudden change of temperature that would check their growth. For gardeners without cold frames, putting plants outdoors during the day in a sheltered, not too sunny spot and bringing them undercover at night will have the same effect.

Later in the Spring, once the early crops have been harvested, Dennis plants cucumbers and more basil, which will thrive in the warm and humid atmosphere of the frames. As with the rest of his domain, Dennis puts his success with the cold frames down to a regular Autumn application of farmyard manure (according to the rotation) to keep the soil fertile. He has few problems with pests, other than the occasional slug.

Tucked away behind the ornamental greenhouses, there is a small, workman-like glasshouse where he does much of his plant raising. Seeds are sown in Highgrove's own seed medium (see The Blueprint, page 158). Most will need only protection from frost to germinate, but for tender plants, like tomatoes and cucumbers, he uses a heated sand bench in one of the ornamental glasshouses. Once germinated, these plants are removed from the propagator, potted up, and after a few days moved to Dennis's glasshouse.

*After sowing seed, Dennis will use a heated sand bench to germinate the early vegetable plants for the Walled Garden. Once the seedlings appear, they are potted up and moved to a frost-free greenhouse to grow on.*

*The cold frames are invaluable for growing early crops of spinach, basil and celery and for hardening-off young plants before they are moved to their permanent positions in the garden.*

In Spring, there is a production line of seedlings emerging from the Highgrove glasshouses to be hardened off and planted out. Successional sowing is an essential technique in every organic garden. Sowing regular batches of seeds extends cropping through the entire growing season. As a general rule, the next batch of seeds should be sown as the previous seedlings are planted out in the garden. In a small garden this can still be done by sowing fewer seeds and planting shorter rows.

Once the main sowing season is over, Dennis plants tomatoes in his glasshouse. His preferred varieties are all tried and tested. 'Shirley' bears heavy crops of fine-flavoured, regular-sized fruit (and has the advantage of being resistant to *Fusarium*, *Cladosporium* and tomato mosaic virus), while 'Gardener's Delight' and 'Sweet 100' bear long trusses of delicious cherry-type tomatoes. They are grown as cordons; this method involves routinely pinching out the non-fruiting side-shoots to stimulate the plants to produce fruit rather than masses of foliage. Left to its own devices, a tomato plant will form a bush that sprawls across the ground; cordons are far more manageable, especially under glass. Manure water is Dennis's favoured tomato feed. This is made by suspending a sack of well-rotted manure in a tub of water and using the resultant liquid as a feed.

## Permanent planting

Within the Walled Garden there are apples, pears, damsons, plums and acid (Morello) cherries. At present there is only one sweet cherry, although it is planned to introduce more. The trees are all 25 years old; a gift from the Worshipful Company of Fruiterers which has now reached its full mature glory. The trees were planted in threes to make sure of a reasonable crop from each variety, and by selecting a dozen different apple varieties the picking and eating season has been extended. The damson trees have proved especially productive; annually each tree is weighed down by more than a hundredweight of fruit which is harvested to make Duchy Originals jams.

A tunnel of apple trees, underplanted with hellebores and backed by sweet briar roses, arches over the gravel path that leads from one end of the garden to the other. Training the trees on a framework (espaliering) over the path creates a space that would not normally be productive. It produces a significant crop and is a delight to walk through when the trees are smothered in blossom. Similarly, each year, two arched tunnels are formed from hazel and willow wands, one fragrant and colourful with sweet peas, and the other green and mysterious and dangling with runner beans.

Always keen to try something new, Prince Charles has recently planted four olive trees (a present from Italian friends) in the centre of each bed in the warmest

ABOVE: *Decorative borders line the path which leads to the gazebo. They are planted with a colourful mixture of fruit trees, shrubs, herbs, annuals and half-hardy plants and further embellished with four giant willow tepees.*

LEFT: *At the centre of the Walled Garden is the dipping pool. Such pools were traditionally used for filling watering cans and water carts. The path that surrounds the pool is edged with low-growing herbs and a rosemary hedge.*

quarter of the garden. They have been flowering quite happily, but it remains to be seen whether they can be persuaded to fruit.

More fruit trees are trained against the 12-foot walls, with sour cherries on the shady North-facing walls, and pears, apples and plums taking advantage of the warmth and protection that the sunnier walls provide. Interestingly, the South-facing wall has capping stones that overhang it by about 6 inches. Originally peaches and nectarines would have been planted against this wall and the overhang provided additional shelter and a fixing point from which to suspend protective nets when the fruit was ripening. They have not been replanted here for a number of reasons: most importantly, they are too labour intensive, need protection from frost and they are prone to disease. Climbing roses and other scented climbers grow alongside wall-trained fruit trees, all underplanted with shrubs, herbaceous perennials, herbs and vegetables.

The decorative elements in a kitchen garden play an essential role; they enhance the surroundings and the flowers attract beneficial insects and pollinators. Birds will visit a pond, fountain or birdbath and use the trees, hedges and topiary for shelter and nesting places. They earn their keep by helping the organic gardener to control pests.

Either side of the central path, running at right angles to the apple tunnel, are the herbaceous borders which are a traditional element of a kitchen garden. Here, though, there isn't the usual emphasis on herbaceous perennials. The intention is to provide as much colour as possible through the visitor season, which lasts from April to October, by using a mixture of fruit trees, shrubs, herbs, annuals and tender half-hardy perennials. Four giant hazel and willow tepees punctuate these borders, wreathed in golden hops, runner beans and the highly decorative, violet-flowered and podded, lab-lab beans.

There is a strong topiary presence within the garden in the form of the box edging, This is kept to a minimum elsewhere and limited to four clipped yew cylinders and ten box balls.

The asparagus beds fall within the permanent planting. One of the beds, planted with the traditional variety 'Connover's Colossal', is now more than 20 years old, while 'Grolim', a highly productive and uniform variety, was planted in the other bed five years ago. The "no picking after the 20th of June" rule is strictly enforced to ensure high yields and with more than a thousand spears picked in the most recent season, this strictness is amply rewarded. In the Autumn, when the asparagus foliage turns yellow, it is cut down close to ground level and the beds are hand weeded, then dressed with well-rotted manure. Carefully tended, an asparagus bed can go on indefinitely. If a bed is infested with perennial weeds, it is covered with black plastic. The asparagus spears are strong enough to force their way through, but the weeds, deprived of light, die if the plastic is replaced annually for two or three years when the foliage is cut down.

## Seasonal planting

The emphasis in the kitchen garden is to grow the fruit and vegetables most useful to the Highgrove chefs, who are looking for quality, variety and seasonality. Prince Charles has long championed the benefits of eating foods appropriate to the season, so seasonality is central to the planting in the Walled Garden.

Dennis Brown is the genius of this place. He was taught to garden by his father and has always gardened organically, with a deep and intuitive understanding of the soil and plants. Before he came to Highgrove he was the whipper-in for the Beaufort Hunt and gardening was his hobby. He swept the board at every show he entered and was legendary for his prize-winning vegetables. Dennis was recommended to Prince Charles as the man to take on the Walled Garden. Now in his seventies, he has the energy of a man half his age and works tirelessly to make sure that the kitchen garden remains consistently productive.

Dennis leaves the Walled Garden at the end of the day and starts work on his own plot, where he spend his evenings cultivating the vegetables he hopes will trounce all-comers at the local shows. His devotion to farmyard manure as the key to good vegetable growing is in evidence in his plots, which are a now good 2 feet above their original level.

Like children, plants need as good an environment as possible to grow in or they will not thrive. The soil in the Walled Garden is about as good as it gets, which makes preparation quite simple. In January or February, depending on the weather and conditions underfoot, Dennis spreads two-year-old composted manure over the surface of those beds scheduled for enrichment (according to the crop rotation plans). This is then rotavated into the top 4 inches of the soil. The box hedging and the many cordon apple trees at the edges of the beds are given particularly generous quantities of manure so they don't rob the surrounding soil of the fertility that is needed for the vegetables. Unusually for an organically managed garden, green manures aren't used. David explains, "There's no harm if the garden is well managed. We dig in residues and then plant catch crops (a quick-growing crop) whenever a space comes available."

The early sowings are done under glass, but as soon as the soil has warmed up, Dennis starts direct sowing. In general, the rows are oriented North/South to take full advantage of the sun and avoid crops shading their neighbours, although this isn't always the case in the triangular beds, where planting is a combination of rows planted parallel to the box hedging, and block planting filling the awkward shape that remains.

Crop rotation is an essential tool for the organic gardener. Just as our bodies need a mixed diet to stay healthy, so the garden needs to grow a rotating selection of crops to avoid a build-up of pests and diseases. Grow any vegetable (with a few exceptions) in the same place, over and over again, and the crop will get smaller

*Prince Charles enjoys Brussels sprouts, so several varieties are planted to ensure cropping over a long period. Dennis plants them into a V-shaped trench and earths them up as they grow to prevent them falling over.*

*"My general rule is don't grow it unless you use it."*

HEAD GARDENER DAVID HOWARD

# Three-year rotation plan for the vegetable garden

**Top-left plot**

YEAR ONE
Onions (Alliacae)
YEAR TWO
Brussels (Brassicas)
YEAR THREE
Peas (Legumes)

YEAR ONE
Carrots (Roots)
YEAR TWO
Leeks (Alliacae)
YEAR THREE
Peas (Legumes)

YEAR ONE
Potatoes
YEAR TWO
Peas (Legumes)
YEAR THREE
Brussels (Brassicas)

YEAR ONE
Brussels (Brassicas)
YEAR TWO
Carrots or Onions
(Roots or Alliacae)
YEAR THREE
Potatoes

**Top-right plot**

YEAR ONE
Leeks (Alliacae)
YEAR TWO
Broad beans (Legumes)
YEAR THREE
Cabbage or Cauliflower
(Brassicas)

YEAR ONE
French beans (Legumes)
YEAR TWO
Potatoes
YEAR THREE
Broad beans
(Legumes)

Asparagus

YEAR ONE
Heritage seed
YEAR TWO
Onions (Alliacae)

**Bottom-left plot**

YEAR ONE
Carrots (Roots)
YEAR TWO
Brussels (Brassicas)
YEAR THREE
Carrots (Roots)

Asparagus

YEAR ONE
Lettuce and Spinach
YEAR TWO
Cabbage or
Cauliflower (Brassicas)
YEAR THREE
Leeks

YEAR ONE
Heritage seeds
YEAR TWO
Brussels (Brassicas)
YEAR THREE
Peas (Legumes)

**Bottom-right plot**

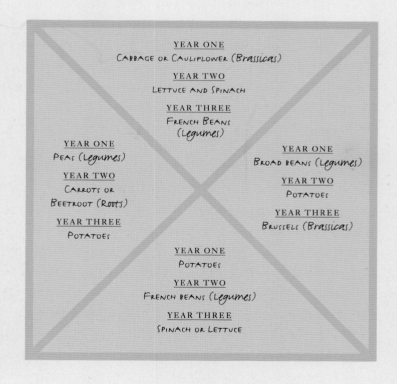

YEAR ONE
Cabbage or Cauliflower (Brassicas)
YEAR TWO
Lettuce and Spinach
YEAR THREE
French Beans
(Legumes)

YEAR ONE
Peas (Legumes)
YEAR TWO
Carrots or
Beetroot (Roots)
YEAR THREE
Potatoes

YEAR ONE
Broad beans (Legumes)
YEAR TWO
Potatoes
YEAR THREE
Brussels (Brassicas)

YEAR ONE
Potatoes
YEAR TWO
French beans (Legumes)
YEAR THREE
Spinach or Lettuce

*In the Walled Garden at Highgrove there is a complex rotation that
encompasses 18 beds, many of which produce two crops a year, as well as catch
crops such as lettuce, radishes and spinach.*

and the problems get larger. All good gardeners use crop rotation to get the best use out of their vegetable plots.

Crop rotation is based on grouping together vegetables from the same plant family because they generally require similar conditions. The garden is divided into plots or beds that host each family in turn. Rotations vary and need not be followed slavishly, but making sure that beds do not grow the same crop two years in a row cuts down on pest and disease problems. Adopting a systematic approach also makes it easier to keep track of what gets planted where.

A typical four-year rotation starts with a generously manured plot, half of which is planted with potatoes and half with brassicas. When the potatoes have been harvested, over-Wintering members of the onion family follow in the Autumn. The next Spring it's the turn of squashes, pumpkins and courgettes. Peas and beans are planted in the third year and finally, in year four, root vegetables, which would fork and distort if they were grown in richer soil.

In the Walled Garden at Highgrove there is a complex rotation that encompasses 18 beds, many of which produce two crops a year as well as catch crops such as lettuce, radishes and spinach. It is a system devised and understood solely by Dennis and is based on both a lifetime's wisdom and reliably fertile soil, which means that he can vary the rotation in a way that would muddle less experienced gardeners. Over three years, one bed grows potatoes, followed by peas, then brassicas, while an adjoining bed starts with onions, then brassicas and finally peas. This demonstrates that it is the rotation that is important, while the order in which plants follow one another can be more flexible, provided the requirements of each vegetable family are met.

THERE ARE SOME KEY POINTS TO REMEMBER.

– Potatoes and brassicas need soil that has been newly enriched with good-quality compost or manure.
– Members of the onion family (leeks, garlic and shallots, as well as onions) like to grow in soil that was manured for a previous crop.
– Squashes, pumpkins and courgettes need plenty of humus to help keep the soil moist, but too rich a soil will grow leaves at the expense of fruit.
– Peas and beans also require an input of humus rather than manure.
– Root vegetables are best grown at the end of a rotation.

When David Howard was appointed head gardener he asked Dennis where he could find the rotation plans. Dennis tapped his head. "They're all in here," he replied. David follows a similar method in the rest of the garden, confiding, "It's the way we head gardeners keep control." The rest of us may prefer (and need) to keep a written record.

*Potatoes are chitted (allowed to sprout) in a frost-free place before they are planted out in trenches. Chitting gets the potatoes off to a flying start and produces a heavier crop.*

Dennis's selection of vegetable seeds is based first and foremost on the preferences and requirements of Prince Charles and his chefs. Leeks and Brussels sprouts are great favourites, so he grows five varieties of sprouts, including a purple variety, and two crops of leeks. Pink Fir Apple and Anya potatoes are also much in demand.

Varieties are selected for their flavour, natural vigour and as much disease resistance as possible. It is easy to be seduced by seed catalogues into buying all sorts of extraordinary vegetables and ending up with not enough of the essentials. Knowledgeable gardeners like Dennis concentrate on growing an abundance of traditional vegetables. (See The Blueprint, pages 159–60 for the Highgrove Walled Garden seed list.)

Organic gardeners need to be discriminating when it comes to choosing seed varieties. While old-fashioned varieties certainly have their place, good disease resistance and suitability to the climate and locality are also key considerations. Dennis routinely trials seeds and ends up with a cross-section of commercial, traditional and new varieties, as well as his own saved seed from runner beans and sweet peas.

As part of this cross-section, each year one of the triangular beds in the Walled Garden is used to grow heritage seeds. Prince Charles is Patron of the Heritage Seed Library, an organization which acts as guardian of the old vegetable varieties that are increasingly hard to find elsewhere. Their aim is to keep these mainly European varieties available and distribute them free to members, despite European Union regulations that attempt to standardize and limit the seeds we can grow. Members allow a percentage of the crop to set seed and return this to

*Dennis puts netting in place to protect peas from damage by wood pigeons. A hungry flock will quickly strip the plants, so prevention is better than cure.*

*A prolific runner bean tunnel leads to one of the arbours at the centre of the four quadrants of the vegetable garden. Like the apple arches, this is a way of making otherwise dead space productive.*

the library or swap it with other members. By keeping old varieties alive the library helps to maintain vital biodiversity.

When selecting seeds, where possible buy those that have been bred organically. They will have been selected by the seed company as being suitable for organic cultivation. Catalogues aimed at organic growers do their best to source a comprehensive range, but supply is limited and where there is nothing suitable they will offer tried-and-tested varieties with good disease resistance instead.

Dennis is modest about his vegetable growing techniques, considering that there is little out of the ordinary in what he does. However, his solution for preventing top-heavy Brussels sprouts leaning over is worth emulating. The young plants are transplanted into the bottom of a V-shaped trench, and as they grow their stems are progressively earthed up and will root into the trenches, holding them firmly in place.

## Maintenance

Being an organic gardener means taking an holistic and philosophical approach to pests and diseases. The intention is not to eliminate problems, but to create a balance that keeps them under control, while not spoiling the garden's beauty or productivity.

At Highgrove, this approach is at the heart of the management of every part of the garden. The soil is healthy, which in turn produces strong, vigorous plants with an improved ability to cope with diseases. In addition, by using home-produced compost and making their own potting mixtures, the problems of imported soil-borne diseases are greatly reduced. Ideally, this type of closed system is something to which every organic gardener should aspire.

But even the best system can't guarantee complete freedom from disease. Like many gardens, Highgrove has had to contend with an attack of box blight that has left some of the hedges in the Walled Garden looking brown and patchy. Reluctant to pull out the affected hedging and start again, the gardeners have tried a new method of controlling this fungal disease. They believe that poor air circulation creates ideal conditions for the fungus to spread, which is why it often spreads from the centre of the hedge outwards. To get air to the central area a deep U-shaped channel is cut along the top of the hedge and all the infected leaves and stems are carefully removed. The new growth looks green and healthy and work is now underway to reduce the height and width of the hedges by some 50 per cent and give them pointed rather than flat tops. This will remove the dense centre of the hedge where the fungus establishes itself and will also help the hedges to shed water – another preventative measure.

In general, problems with pests and diseases are few and far between in Highgrove's productive gardens. Carrot root fly does occur occasionally, but selecting resistant varieties helps, as does delaying the main sowing until late July to avoid the root fly life cycle. Where earlier plantings take place they are covered with fleece to keep the fly at bay. Flea beetle, the scourge of many gardens, has never been seen, but David Howard does have excellent advice for other gardeners on how to combat it. He advises, "Plant your brassicas in the shade; flea beetles love sunshine. Farmers noticed that plants growing in full sunshine were badly affected, while those in the shade of a hedge were untouched." However, both shade and competing roots can affect crop growth, so shade-netting is probably the best solution. There is canker on some of the fruit trees, but it is pruned out and this seems to keep it under control. When doing this, it is essential to clean tools afterwards to avoid transferring the canker to a healthy tree.

Before any planting took place in the restored Walled Garden, care was taken to rid it of all perennial weeds. This has paid great dividends; now all that is necessary is regular hand weeding and hoeing to control annual weeds.

*"It's a matter of taking the rough with the smooth, no two years are the same. We are working with Nature to 'manage' pests and diseases, not to eliminate them…"*

HRH THE PRINCE OF WALES

LEFT: *Box blight has proved to be quite a problem at Highgrove, but the gardeners have found that by removing and burning all affected wood and leaves and opening up the centre of the hedge to improve air circulation, the hedges are regenerating.*

ABOVE: *Cutting the box hedges right back may seem like radical treatment and it has left the garden looking a bit bare, but it is worthwhile to save the hedges. The new growth will be trimmed to a point rather than a flat top to prevent a recurrence.*

As tempting as it is to rush into planting, an organic gardener must clear the soil of perennial weeds, or forever struggle to extract them from all the inconvenient places they choose to grow. If the soil is seriously infested, the best solution is to cover it with a black plastic sheet, old hessian-backed carpet or porous landscaping fabric and leave this in place for at least a couple of seasons before removing it. The advantage of carpet or landscaping fabric is that it doesn't smother the soil organisms along with the weeds. None of these options is attractive to look at, but a thick layer of woodchip can be used as a decorative mulch and dug in to add humus to the soil once it is uncovered.

As with the other elements that make up a garden, the materials used to support, train and display plants are most pleasing when they are in harmony with their surroundings. In the Walled Garden, everything is natural, sustainable and biodegradable, sourced from within the estate and tailor-made for the plants. Coppiced hazel is used for bean poles, and also for pea sticks to support peas and anything else that might flop. The sweet pea and runner bean tunnels are formed from hazel uprights positioned either side of a path, with willow wands bent to form the arch above them. These subtle and practical supports soon disappear

LEFT: *One of the tasks that Prince Charles likes to get involved with is laying the estate's hedges. Not only does it create an attractive stock-proof barrier, it also provides useful material to use for plant supports in the garden.*

BELOW: *Dennis and Marion make the tunnels that will support the sweet peas and runner beans. The uprights are made from coppiced hazel and the arches from more pliable willow wands – both of which are harvested on the Highgrove Estate.*

RIGHT: *This group of hornbeam saplings has been trained to form an arbour with its own seat. In time the sapling seat will be strong enough to sit upon. Regular pruning will maintain the shape.*

under foliage and flowers as the plants grow, but until this happens they have a pleasingly rustic appearance. At the end of the season, as plants die back, the beanpoles and pea sticks are removed. Those that are in good condition are stored for the following year; any broken ones are recycled by being chipped.

In the borders, the four giant tepees supporting golden hops and climbing beans are constructed by the gardeners from hazel, ash and willow. Each one is 8 feet high and 6 feet in diameter. Handmade *in situ*, their individual idiosyncrasies give them a charm that would be lacking from something that was made in a fixed and uniform way. The individuality of a garden comes not only from the owner but also from the people who work there and play their part in shaping a garden. Throughout the garden, jute string, with its subtle natural colour and biodegradability, is used to tie in plants or bind supports.

Where space allows, it is worth following the Highgrove example by growing your own plant supports. Once established, three or four hazel bushes will provide a good supply of pea sticks and beanpoles, provided they are coppiced regularly. Alternatively, you should be able to buy locally grown bean poles and pea sticks. There is an increasing number of small-scale managed woodlands where these materials are harvested and sold. Check www.allotmentforestry.com for suppliers.

ABOVE AND RIGHT: *The gardeners at Highgrove learn how to work with willow and hazel so that they can make plant supports* in situ. *Constructed in Spring, the supports quickly disappear beneath the growing plants.*

LEFT: *Early each year the climbers that form the arbours are untied, pruned and repositioned to form neat domes of green. By the end of Summer they will be covered with exuberant explosions of foliage that conceal the order beneath.*

# Satellite gardens

TUCKED UP AGAINST the exterior wall, on the Southern side of the Walled Garden, are a number of productive satellite gardens where fruit, flowers and additional vegetables are grown. The Cutting Garden and the Model Fruit Garden flank the path that leads from the South gate of the Walled Garden, while beyond them, on the other side of the Rose Walk, there are various patches where vegetables such as squashes, courgettes, pumpkins, rhubarb and Swiss chard can be grown without using up valuable space in the Walled Garden.

The Model Fruit Garden is an example of how to combine orchard fruit and soft fruit in a small area. The use of dwarfing rootstocks and restricted methods of cultivation keeps the wall-trained pear trees small. However, the blackcurrants and gooseberries are planted at the traditional, and generous, 6-foot spacings. They are more productive this way and the good air circulation between the bushes has eliminated disease problems.

This piece of ground was a remnant of an earlier nursery that had become infested with bindweed and ground elder. It took seven years to clear, but the majority of both weeds have now been removed through a combination of mulching with black plastic and double digging. The aim here is the same as in the main garden: to supply reasonable quantities of fruit and grow several varieties of each to ensure continuity.

The favoured South-facing wall is very warm and could have been used to grow peaches or nectarines. However, pears, which are more useful and easier to grow, were planted instead. Part of their role is to provide ingredients for products in the shop, so those with the best preserving qualities were selected. With the exception of 'Conference,' all of the others are French varieties: 'William's Bon Chrétien', 'Peradel', 'Doyenné du Comice', 'Delbard d'Automne', 'Beurré Hardy', 'Delbard Delice', 'Delbard Gourmande', 'Super Comice Delbard', 'Duchesse d'Angoulême' and 'Grand Champion'. The wall is high enough for them to be trained as vertical cordons – the trees are grown as single stems with all side shoots cut back to encourage fruiting buds. They are tied to ash rods that have been harvested from the estate's hedges. Bamboo canes are usually used for this purpose, but ash rods make a good home-grown substitute. The pears are underplanted with gold-lace polyanthus, a wonderful foil for the Spring blossom.

The beds in the fruit garden are planted with strawberries, raspberries, blackcurrants and gooseberries. There are four varieties of strawberry: 'Florence' and 'Symphony', which Prince Charles considers to be the best flavoured of the modern varieties, as well as 'Elsanta' and 'Marshmallow', a fruit rejected by commercial growers because it bruises easily, but is of exceptional flavour. The strawberries do not require a great deal of attention other than bedding them in straw as the fruit begins to ripen. The foliage is cut off in late Winter and plants

*Restrictive pruning methods are used on the wall-trained pear trees to maximize productivity and minimize growth. Side shoots are pruned back each Winter to encourage fruiting buds to form.*

RIGHT: *The wall is tall enough to allow the pears to be trained as vertical cordons. Instead of the usual bamboo canes, the trees are tied to ash rods that have been cut from the estate's hedges.*

BELOW: *The South-facing wall is very warm and radiates the sun's heat, creating ideal conditions for blossom to set and form fruit. This wall could have been used for peaches and nectarines, but they are more work and less reliable than pears.*

*"I think that William Lawson probably sums up my view of the productive garden in a quotation from 'A New Orchard and Garden', London [1626]: 'Husbandry maintaines the world, how ancient, how profitable, how pleasant it is, how many secrets of Nature it doth containe, how loved [sic].' It is gratifying to know that this pleasurable husbandry encompasses the organic, local and seasonal aspects of food production."*

HRH THE PRINCE OF WALES

are replaced if there is any sign of failure, but no compost is added to the soil and they are largely left to their own devices.

'Glen Ample' is grown as a Summer-fruiting raspberry, followed by 'Joan J' for Autumn fruit. 'Glen Ample' has the advantage of having spineless canes, which make the deep red, tasty raspberries easy to pick. Summer-fruiting canes are cut down as they finish fruiting and strong new growth is selected and tied in place to fruit next year. Autumn varieties are cut to the ground in early Winter. New canes will grow the following year.

Late-flowering blackcurrants 'Ben Conan' and 'Ben Sarek' have been chosen to avoid the possibility of frost damage. They bear large fruit on compact, mildew-resistant bushes. Growing alongside them are old-fashioned gooseberry varieties 'Leveller' and 'Invicta'. 'Leveller' is reputed to have the best flavour of all and 'Invicta' is resistant to gooseberry mildew. Common gooseberry sawfly is a persistent pest, but any infestation is dealt with early by checking for caterpillars and picking them off the bushes before they get out of hand.

In an organic system, pests and diseases are best managed by choosing disease-resistant varieties and dealing with problems as early as possible to ensure that they don't get a chance to inflict real damage. This requires a watchful eye.

In Spring, the soil surrounding the plants is spread with manure or compost, depending on what is available at the time. All other areas and the paths are mulched with old carpet topped with 4 inches of woodchip to suppress any remaining perennial weeds. This also conserves moisture, reduces weeding and provides easy access.

As a recent project, the Model Fruit Garden is not yet mature or complete, but it is hoped that it will prove highly productive, especially once the fruit cage has been erected and the pick of the crop is no longer shared with the birds. Some produce can be stored. The Apple Store is a picturesque traditional building that

*During the Autumn and Winter, the Apple Store has an ever-changing selection of fruit, as the different varieties are harvested and stored until they are needed. Careful selection of varieties provides apples from late Summer to late Winter.*

*Expert pruning results in fruit borne close to the main stems of the apple tunnel, which makes harvesting relatively easy. The tunnel also creates welcome shade in Summer and is good use of otherwise unproductive space.*

continues to fulfil its original function. On the upper floor, wooden racks hold carefully arranged rows of apples and pears. Most varieties are stored here for a limited period; ripening times vary, some are best eaten fresh while others will mature in the store. Below, on the ground floor, potatoes, carrots and other root vegetables are kept in cool dark conditions until they are needed. Any of the vegetables from the productive gardens that are surplus to the needs of the house or the Orchard Room needs are sent to the Duchy Home Farm where they are used in the box scheme.

The Cutting Garden is under the guiding hand of florist Sarah Champier. Sarah arrived at Highgrove as a trainee gardener via the WRAGS scheme (see The Blueprint, page 160), but her previous training as a florist has given her the opportunity to combine the two skills.

Before Sarah took over, all the flowers were bought in; now, everything is picked from the gardens during the main cutting season which runs from April to October. This is another example of seeking to implement sustainable practices at Highgrove. The majority of cut flowers sold in Britain are grown abroad, often with a high input of pesticides and inorganic fertilizers, and are transported long distances. It made sense for Highgrove to establish a productive flower garden and become as self-sufficient as possible in cut flowers.

The Cutting Garden flowers are started from organic seed, raised in the greenhouses and cold frames and then planted out in the garden. There are 16 beds measuring 8 by 10 feet. They contain a mixture of annual, biennial and

LEFT: *A Green Man – made out of moss by Sarah the florist – is comfortably seated among the flowers and foliage in the Cutting Garden.*

RIGHT AND BELOW: *Sarah works hard to make the Cutting Garden attractive as well as productive. Instead of flowers being planted in straight rows they are grouped together in square beds, which are just as practical to manage.*

perennial flowers interspersed with fragrant English Roses, as well as foliage plants including pittosporum, *Euonymus japonicus*, fatsia, cardoons and euphorbia. (See The Blueprint, page 161 for Sarah's list of the plants that are the backbone of the Cutting Garden.) The paths are mulched in the same way as in the fruit garden to suppress the weeds. Against the back wall of the Cutting Garden there are a few old trees that are due to be replaced by more cordon pears.

The garden is quite new so the planting is still evolving. "I planned the layout so it would be pretty and as it matures I hope it will become fabulous and blowsy," says Sarah. Sweet peas are the one cut-flower that Sarah doesn't attempt to grow. She leaves that to Dennis, who harvests all she needs from the sweet pea tunnel in the Walled Garden.

In the Summer months Sarah spends half her time cutting and conditioning the flowers and the other half maintaining the garden. Most of the flowers need staking or supporting to ensure straight stems. She attends the willow-weaving courses which are held regularly for the gardeners so she can make all these supports herself from material gathered on the Highgrove Estate.

Additional foliage and flowers are gathered from other parts of the garden. Sarah explains, "I'm expert at scavenging around the backs of bushes to get the things I need. Because the flower-arranging style is very informal and follows the seasons, I usually only need a few branches or stems of any one thing at a time." Prince Charles particularly loves scented flowers and these are incorporated into arrangements wherever possible, especially in the small vases placed on bedside tables and desks. As well as the flowers for the house, the garden supplies materials for fund-raising events in the Orchard Room and any floral gifts, tributes and posies that may be given by Prince Charles.

# The orchards

As ORCHARDS GO, Highgrove's is quite youthful. There are no venerable trees with craggy bark and gnarled branches amid knee-high drifts of wild flowers. The purpose of this orchard is primarily to be productive with fruit from the trees, eggs from the chickens scratching in the grass, and honey from the bees which pollinate the blossom. All three sit well in this space and eventually time will work its transforming magic.

Twenty-five years ago the orchard consisted of a two-acre paddock conveniently situated next to the productive garden. Half of it was planted with commercial varieties of apple tree (a present from an organization of which the Prince used to be President), while the other half was left as paddock. It soon became apparent that the orchard was producing apples that everyone grew, but in non-commercial quantities. As all surplus fruit is sold to raise funds for some of the countless charities and organizations the Prince supports, it was essential to remedy this.

In 2003, rather than grubbing it all up and starting again, the tops of the trees were removed and they were grafted with pest and disease resistant varieties recommended for organic cultivation. These were selected using Martin Crawford's *Directory of Apple Cultivars*, essential reading for anyone planning to plant an orchard. At present the trees still look rather truncated, but they have started to bear fruit again and will soon regain their normal height and spread. Nine of the original trees escaped radical surgery. These are crab apples, *Malus hupehensis*, which were planted as pollinators for the commercial varieties. Their cherry-like fruits (in appearance, not flavour) are harvested in October and used to make crab apple jelly for the Highgrove shop. Any gardener faced with a mature tree that produces indifferent apples could consider grafting, rather than its

*The flowering cherries were initially planted elsewhere, but failed to thrive in the waterlogged ground. Since they have been moved to the edge of the orchard they have flourished and now bloom prodigiously.*

*A Celtic hedge of interwoven willow forms the boundary of the orchard. Overhanging it there is a cloud of blossom from the row of great white flowering cherries* Prunus *'Taihaku'.*

removal. Once the graft has taken, the substantial root system and trunk will stimulate rapid growth of the new variety. Courses in grafting, where an experienced gardener can learn this skill, are held around the country and can be found on the internet. Alternatively, if you would prefer to employ a professional, visit a local orchard and ask them to recommend someone who could graft your tree for you.

The remaining half of the orchard continued as a paddock until 2005, when it was planted with a range of different tree fruit. The aim is to produce small quantities of high-quality organic fruit for processing and selling in the shop. The new trees include late-flowering apricots 'Bergacot', 'Flavorcot' and 'Tomcot' which have been specially bred for cool climates, French Mirabelle plums 'M. de Nancy', 'Bergeron' and 'Montclar', as well as damsons, quinces, medlars and black mulberries. In addition, sea buckthorn, *Hippophae rhamnoides*, is being grown for its bead-like orange berries which are rich in vitamin C and *Sorbus megalocarpa* for its tiny pear-shaped fruit.

The majority of these fruit trees are half-standards and will be pruned to have open centres. They were planted in generous holes with soil enriched by compost and bonemeal. Once the trees were in position, they were tied to sturdy hazel stakes and the young trunks were protected with rabbit guards. The trees were watered for the first two years and mulched with old carpet covered with several inches of woodchip.

Fruit tree diseases are limited from the outset by selecting varieties that aren't susceptible. Any pests in the orchard are largely dealt with by the chickens. When the birds are first introduced to a fresh area of grass in the orchard, they immediately scratch around the base of the trees and eat all the bugs that lurk beneath. This is natural pest control of the very best sort. Ducks are also excellent slug and snail eliminators in a garden, but they are a magnet for foxes.

Chickens do well in orchards and are excellent for soil fertility. The eggs are organically produced, following Soil Association guidelines, and marketed through the Duchy Home Farm's box scheme. The guidelines stipulate that the flock consists of organically reared birds, fed an organic diet on regularly rotated organic pasture. David Howard is a great chicken enthusiast and is extremely knowledgeable about their breeding and care. The birds are largely traditional breeds such as Marans, Wellsummers and Light Sussex, chosen to produce a variety of egg colours. A natural gap in egg production has been filled by crossing two of these traditional breeds and creating hybrids that have the capacity to lay more eggs over a longer period. As a result there are eggs every week of the year. There is a low spot at the end of October and the beginning of November which is related to the decrease in day length, but David prefers to do without artificial light. "The idea is to encourage rather than enforce," he says. Continuity of production is also helped by hatching the eggs at different dates so that the pullets

LEFT: *The various ponds and water features attract wild ducks to Highgrove. The ducks are welcomed because they are a wonderfully efficient organic way of controlling pests such as slugs and snails.*

ABOVE: *The Orchard is a perfect place to keep chickens. They improve the soil fertility and scratch around in the grass eating all the pests. The chickens are rotated between four paddocks, each of which supports the flock for three months at a time.*

come into lay at different times, although, as chicks need long days to grow, there is a limit to the period when this can be done.

The chickens are hatched elsewhere on the estate. They arrive in the orchard when they are six weeks old and are housed in small enclosed pens. After four to six weeks they are introduced to the main rearing house where they are fed ad lib organic food and water. Once there, they are encouraged to go out and forage for other food within the confines of an electric fence which protects them from predators. The foraging areas consist of four quarter-acre patches, each of which supports the birds (stocked at a rate of 80 to the acre) for three months. They remain in the rearing house until a month before they are due to start laying at six to seven months old.

At this point they are moved on to the laying house, where they soon start to produce Highgrove's prize-winning eggs. The hens lay for a year and are then relocated. This isn't an anodyne euphemism for culling; they are moved to the decorative pen near the house, from where some will be used as breeding stock and others will be sold to "happy homes".

The Soil Association view is that healthy birds can resist pathogens. To maintain the health of the Highgrove chickens, the buildings are thoroughly cleaned and disinfected during the Winter months when there is a lull in rearing. One-way movement of stock is another measure that keeps disease rates low.

Bees are also important in the Highgrove orchard. On a visit to Slovenia, Prince Charles was presented with a traditional wooden bee house. The great advantage of this structure is that it is mobile, allowing all the hives to be moved to another location in one go. All the colonies are housed beneath one roof, protected from the cold in Winter and heat in Summer. The ten hives are slotted alongside one another in a double row, rather like a miniature apartment block, and their facades are decorated with charming paintings of Slovenian folk tales. A door in the side of the house reveals that behind the hives there is a veritable honey factory, with spare frames, an extractor and other useful equipment stored just where it is needed. The principal difference in looking after bees in this type of building is that each frame is removed as soon as it is filled, which keeps the bees busy all year. In conventional British hives, the frames are left in place until all are filled.

The bees are wonderful pollinators and productive in terms of the honey crop. However, because DEFRA (Department of Food and Rural Affairs) requires that all bees are treated for the virulent veroa mite, the honey cannot be sold as organic. It is the only Highgrove crop that isn't.

There is another, smaller orchard at Highgrove in front of the Carpet Garden. It contains a collection of the oldest and rarest apples in the country and was a gift from the Brogdale Horticultural Trust, home to the National Fruit Collection (see The Blueprint, page 162). This gift was greatly appreciated by Prince Charles, not only because it gave him a fascinating collection of trees but also because of its role in the conservation of genetic material. (The sale of Brogdale by the Ministry of Agriculture, Fisheries and Food in 1991 potentially put this important collection of 2,300 varieties of apple, built up since Roman times, at risk. Prince Charles felt passionately that this unique and irreplaceable pool of genetic material should be preserved for future generations, and provided the funding for the newly formed Brogdale Horticultural Trust to purchase the land and collection.)

The trees fruit well and the harvested apples go to Highgrove's Home Farm for selling at farmers' markets in Cirencester. Among the many successful varieties grown in this orchard is a huge green cooker called 'Devonshire Buckland'. Although it only keeps for about three weeks it is well worth including in an orchard. Another recommendation is a local Gloucestershire russet apple called 'Hunt's Duke of Gloucester' that is reputed to have been grown from a seed of the now lost 'Nonpareil'. The fruit has a distinct flavour of pineapple.

The orchard trees are underplanted with 'Imperial Gem' lavender, which looks very attractive. This variety has flowers of a similar colour to 'Hidcote' but a bushier, more upright habit, without the tendency to fall apart and look untidy.

LEFT: *The small orchard in front of the Carpet Garden contains a collection of the oldest and rarest apples in the country, given to Prince Charles by the Brogdale Horticultural Trust, home to the National Fruit Collection.*

ABOVE: *This traditional wooden bee house was given to the Prince when he visited Slovenia. It houses ten hives, which are slotted alongside one another and decorated with paintings of Slovenian folk tales.*

3

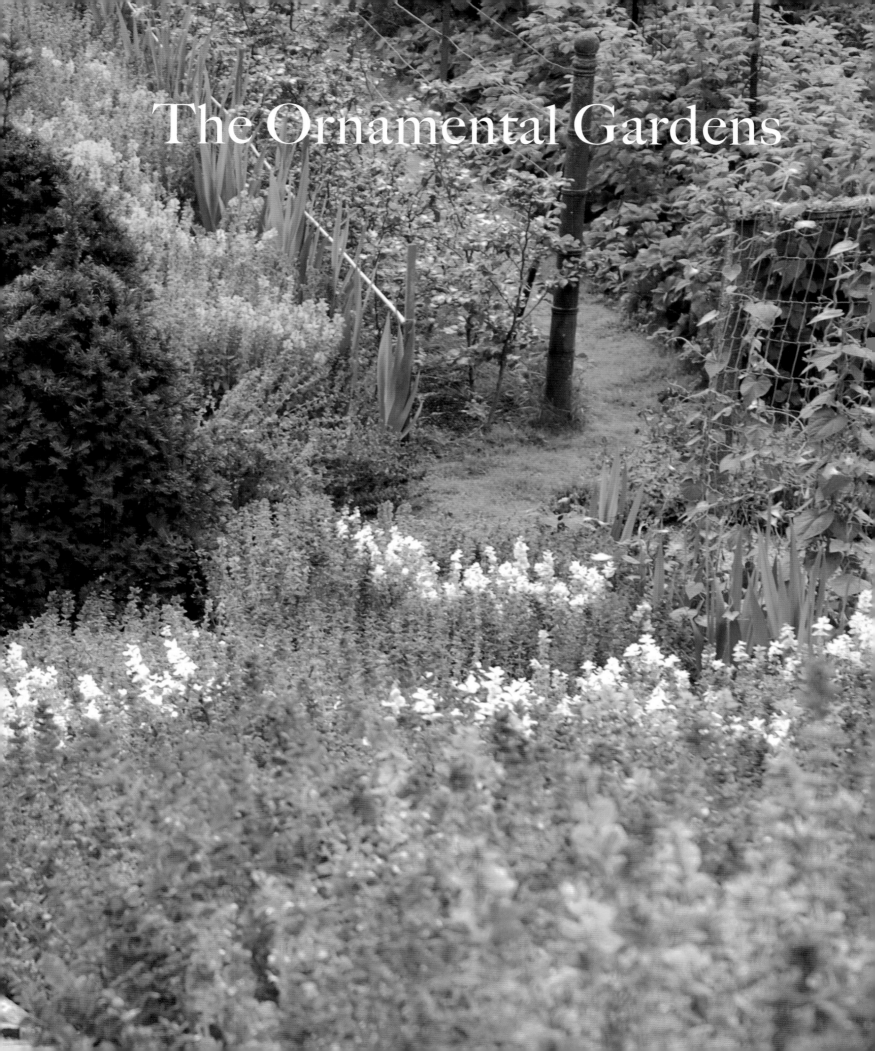

The Ornamental Gardens

*"For me, the garden is an expression of what I hold dear – whether of harmony or humour – and it is in the ornamental gardens that this element can be exploited."*

HRH THE PRINCE OF WALES

# The structure of the gardens
## *Hedges, trees and topiary*

PRINCE CHARLES'S PERSONAL TASTE, particular outlook and philosophy have created these gardens. While various designers have made their contribution, it is always with his involvement and approval. Although some practical measures have had to be taken to accommodate the thousands of visitors who come to Highgrove each year, this remains first and foremost a private garden. It was created primarily to please its owner, but also to give pleasure to visitors and arouse their interest. It has also been a means for raising money for many of the causes and organizations supported by Prince Charles. The gardens encompass great diversity, from the Carpet Garden with its Islamic influences through to the highly ornamental, but functional, traditional Walled Garden.

Twenty-six years ago, when Prince Charles first viewed Highgrove, much of the garden was a blank canvas with very little that was worth retaining. First to be addressed was the structure. This was to be a combination of the best features of the inherited design and layout, coupled with new hedging and trees that would be sympathetically integrated with the existing planting – and incorporate various sculptures, arches and gateways.

Two existing features were central to the new design, a magnificent mature cedar of Lebanon, which dominated the formal garden, and a double row of irregularly shaped golden yews flanking a gravel path leading from the West door of the house to a small formal pond. Rather than remove the somewhat unprepossessing yews, Prince Charles chose to incorporate them into the new garden by topiarizing them to create more interesting shapes.

When planning any garden it is essential to look at the existing trees and hedges and to decide whether they are worth retaining. Provided they are healthy, even if unkempt and overgrown, they may be retrievable. The restoration of an old hedge may well be preferable to its removal and replacement. If fed and

*Topiary, hedges and trees decorate, define and enclose the different areas of the garden, giving them their own character. Little of today's planting existed when Prince Charles first arrived at Highgrove.*

*Close to the house, the hedges and topiary are at their most formal. They are kept neatly trimmed to create a setting that matches the classical formality of the house.*

watered when cut back, it will soon regenerate and need far less cosseting than a new hedge. Well-managed mature planting gives a garden character and should not be removed lightly.

At the same time as the rejuvenation of the golden yews was taking place, a new yew hedge was planted to enclose the formal garden. Yew was chosen because it is a classic plant that has been used for hundreds of years to create structure in English gardens. Early on, while the hedges were establishing, they were fed with farmyard manure and the organic fertilizer, fish, blood and bone, and were also watered regularly. There is a perception that yew is a slow-growing plant, but with this treatment it matures quickly, reaching a height of 8 feet in ten years. However, it does require a well-drained soil and will fail to thrive and eventually die in waterlogged conditions. There are many reasons for choosing yew. First, it is a British native that will give a garden a solid and dependable dark green backdrop. Also it is long lived, is a good habitat for wildlife and it takes clipping and extreme cutting back with no adverse affects. Hedge planting was followed by the decision to flank the golden yews with a pleached hornbeam hedge in a series of rectangles. Pleaching is a method of training by intertwining the lateral branches of trees that have usually been planted in a straight line. The branches fuse together as if holding hands. Along these laterals, short spurs (side branches) grow leaves, giving a raised, hedge-like appearance.

As with many garden plans, things didn't turn out quite as intended. The laterals failed to fuse together, so this has become what might more accurately be described as a stilt hedge or hedge-on-legs. This doesn't really matter as the effect is similar to pleaching and it is easier to manage. Failure to fuse can be a problem with hornbeam; lime trees pleach more readily.

The area of cloud-pruned box in the Cottage Garden is the setting for a number of architectural features. Salvaged cathedral-stone bases are topped by sculptures or pots of topiary, and at its centre point there is a vast amphora that rests on its side as if floating on its own box cloud. Originating in Japan, this style of pruning creates gentle undulations and patterns of light and shade in the box. David describes it as "overgrown bonsai that turns the plant into a contrived shape

*Irregular lumps of golden yew lined the Thyme Walk when Prince Charles bought Highgrove. He was advised to remove them, but instead asked his gardeners to prune the yews into interesting shapes.*

*Rectangular plantings of pleached hornbeams create colonnades of tree trunks topped by neatly trimmed hedges. This device reveals the Thyme Walk, and divides it from the rest of the garden.*

*The cloud-pruned box in the Cottage Garden is given a trim. In many ways this is easier to maintain than conventional box hedges, as there are no straight lines that must be followed.*

by managing its growth to create a surreal effect." His description of the box hedging to one side of the main entrance as "an organic box hedge" reveals his preference for the more generous curves that can be created by shaping a mature specimen. The advantage of cloud-pruning is that it gives a softer and less rigid effect and, in many ways, is easier to maintain than a geometrically trimmed hedge. Where box blight is a persistent problem *Ilex crenata* or *Ligustrum japonicum* are possible alternatives, although the ligustrum is not fully hardy and should only be considered in warm, sheltered areas. The Prince, however, much prefers box and believes the problems can be overcome by cutting back the affected areas and foliar feeding with liquid seaweed to give the plants a boost. He advises, "The essential thing is to plant the most resistant variety – usually *Buxus sempervirens*".

Hedgecutting takes place over three months of the year, from July to October. It begins with box, then moves on to beech, followed by yew and finally hornbeam. The aim is to cut the yew in the current season when growth slows and the terminal buds have not quite formed, usually towards the end of August or early September.

There are two approaches to clipping yew. Clip in April when the hedge is actively growing and you will have a uniform structure for a short time, followed by something shaggier for the greater part of the year. Clip in August as growth slows and you will have a shaggy hedge from May to August, but it will be tidily clipped for the rest of the year. This is the preferred method at Highgrove where the neat outlines make a significant contribution to the Winter garden. It is also a more wildlife-friendly regime; in April there is the danger of disturbing nesting birds.

Most of the work is done with electric hedge-trimmers which are used for the sides and other large flat areas of hedging, but the more intricate tops and finials are done by hand. Traditionally yew hedges slope 15 to 20 degrees outwards

towards the ground (this is called a "batter") to allow light to reach right to the base, but the hedges at Highgrove are straight-edged and show no signs of suffering as a result. An additional feature that Prince Charles had always wanted to incorporate into the hedges is the series of windows, cut through the yew at regular intervals. Later, when the Prince was looking for a suitable home for a series of bronze busts of himself (gifts from the sculptors), these windows suggested themselves as an ideal solution. As a joke, the Prince thought the Sundial Garden, where the windows with the busts are situated, should be renamed the "Ego Garden".

For the past six years, the gardeners have collected the yew trimmings and sent them for processing into Taxol, a cancer treatment. However, a synthetic form (about which the Prince has reservations) has recently been developed and the demand for this plant remedy may soon disappear.

Trees that were planted before Prince Charles's arrival have been retained where they contribute to the overall effect in the garden. In particular, there is a plane tree at the bottom of the main lawn, as well as a Tree of Heaven, *Ailanthus altissima*, an aged ginkgo and several Irish yews. Unfortunately, the cedar of Lebanon is infected with a bracket fungus (*Ganoderma applanatum*), which is eating the heart out of the tree and has caused a gradual die-back of the branches over the past 20 years. This has now been accelerated by the appearance of the dreaded honey fungus, *Armillaria mellea*. This fungus only attacks stressed trees and will have a more rapid effect on the cedar's demise as, weakened by the bracket fungus, it has been stressed for some time. There is no organic way of

PREVIOUS PAGE: *The geometrical and idiosyncratic shapes of the topiarized yew lining the Thyme Walk and the blocks of pleached hornbeam are most evident when viewed from the upper windows of the House.*

ABOVE: *The billowing hummocks of cloud-pruned box in the Cottage Garden are naturalistic and do not need to be kept tightly trimmed. The terracotta pot appears to rest on its own cloud of greenery.*

LEFT: *The formality of the new topiary planted by Prince Charles in the Wildflower Meadow makes a pleasing contrast to the surroundings. Yew responds well to hard pruning and training.*

stopping the progress of honey fungus, but, if caught early enough, it can be contained by using mushroom compost as a mulch. This introduces another fungus, *Trichoderma viridi*, which lives companionably with the edible mushroom fungus in the compost, but will attack honey fungus when it encounters it, slowing and containing its progress.

All trees have a natural lifespan and it is recognized that the cedar is near its end. Eighteen years ago, in preparation for the tree's death, Prince Charles planted a replacement young cedar some distance away on the main lawn. It is growing vigorously and is now 30 feet high, but it will be many years before it reaches a similar stature.

The choice of a tree should take into account the size of the space available and the scale of its surroundings. A tree as grand as the cedar of Lebanon needs a setting where it can be viewed at a distance or its stature will never be fully appreciated. Too big a tree in too small a garden looks out of scale and makes growing other plants more difficult because the roots soak up available water and nutrients while the canopy creates shade. Equally, small trees in large gardens need companions or they look lonely and isolated. Always plant with posterity in mind. Most trees will outlive us and it is only fair that we place them somewhere where they can fulfil their full potential.

Blossom-laden *Malus floribunda* trees on the main lawn signify the arrival of Spring in the ornamental gardens at Highgrove. The small but abundant flowers are deep pink in bud, opening to reveal pale pink petals. Elsewhere, the great white cherry *Prunus* 'Taihaku' has been planted to provide what is reputed to be

*Spring bulbs grow in long grass beneath flowering cherry trees. This is a pleasant contrast to the crisp geometry of the surrounding hedges and topiary. The grass will not be cut until the bulbs have died back, to ensure continued flowering.*

BELOW: *A mixture of climbers on this South-facing wall provides flowers through the Summer months. The honeysuckle will remain in bloom throughout the season and when the vivid blue ceanothus fades, it will be replaced by roses.*

the finest of all cherry blossom. A spreading tree, it bears large, pure white, single flowers among bronze foliage which turns green as the leaves mature. The ground in its original position proved to be too heavy and wet and the tree did not thrive. Rather than leave it there, it was moved close to the new orchard when it was five years old and is now growing well. The beeches in front of the Orchard Room also failed to thrive and have been replaced by a collection of *Pterocarya*, including the Caucasian wing-nut, *Pterocarya fraxinifolia*. These are more tolerant of wet soil and are quite happy with standing water around their roots in Winter.

When a young tree is planted, it may take a year or so to settle in, but after that it should grow steadily. If this doesn't happen, the conditions may be unsuitable and you should consider moving it (while it is dormant) to a better position. Lift as much of the rootball as possible and plant the tree in a generous planting hole that has been enriched with compost and bonemeal. Plant it at the same depth as previously to ensure that the soil level reaches the same point on the tree's trunk. As with any other newly planted tree, it will need watering-in and regular water during the first year until it has re-established itself.

When planting trees during the Winter months, bear in mind that nearby trees may appear light and airy, but come the Summer months there will be a canopy of leaves which may exclude both light and rain. Allow sufficient space for the new tree to grow, without its being crowded out or stunted by its neighbours due to lack of light.

There are many ornamental trees which add seasonal interest in the Highgrove gardens. The amelanchiers on the fringes of the Stumpery Garden are a mass of blossom in the Spring and have brightly coloured foliage in the Autumn. The vibrant colour of *Parrotia persica* is an Autumn highlight in the Cottage Garden, while in the Buttress Garden the vivid crimson foliage of *Euonymus alatus* stands out against the dark green of the yew hedges. In smaller gardens the ideal ornamental trees are those that bear flowers in the Spring, and fruit to feed the birds during the Autumn and Winter months. Rowans, hawthorns and crab apples are all suitable for this purpose.

# Climbers

There are times of the year when the formal facades of Highgrove all but disappear under the rampant growth of climbing plants. The Crimson glory vine, *Vitis coignetiae*, festoons the front of the house and the porch with its extravagant architectural leaves. For three weeks in the Autumn the leaves of this vine are suffused with brilliant colours, ranging from dark purple, through red and orange to yellow.

The other dominant plant which clothes the house isn't actually a climber but a Summer-flowering evergreen magnolia. The *Magnolia grandiflora* was originally planted as a wall shrub on the West side of the house, but it has rather taken over and now completely covers two windows on the ground floor and two on the first floor. If the top had not blown out of it in a gale, it would probably have designs on the top floor windows as well. Prince Charles loves it and has no intention of curbing its enthusiastic growth. It is especially wonderful when the delicious scent from its huge, bowl-shaped cream flowers drifts in through the open windows during the Summer months.

The key to success with climbing plants is to use the appropriate plant for the size and scale of the house. The Crimson glory vine is a wonderful plant where space allows, as are other Highgrove climbers, including the yellow-flowered rose Mermaid, *Wisteria floribunda* and the golden hop, *Humulus lupulus* 'Aureus', but most of these could swamp the average house unless carefully managed. The climbers are supported by horizontal wires fixed to the building with vine eyes. Maintenance is an annual pruning, cutting back and tying in during February or March, with minor adjustments later, and a Spring dressing of garden compost.

With climbing roses, the most essential management is the annual pruning and tying in of branches to establish the framework. This is a vital aspect of growing and displaying them well. In January, the Highgrove gardeners remove all of last year's ties, take out the dead, diseased and dying wood and also remove the previous year's flowered wood. They then thin out the remaining stems before tying them in, in an artistic but natural manner. Selecting disease-resistant varieties and keeping the plants healthy with an annual feed of organic compost avoids diseases, and the large population of birds effectively manages any aphid problem.

*To maintain the impressive annual display of wisteria on the Cottage Garden pergola (top), each side shoot is pruned back to two buds in February. In the final stages of its Autumn transformation the leaves of* Vitis coignetiae *(above) turn from deepest crimson to yellow.*

## Lawns

At Highgrove the green flat areas in the formal gardens are not described as lawns. They are green spaces which are mown regularly, but that's where the similarity to a lawn ends. They are never aerated, fed, weeded or watered and there is quite a lot of the moss which the Prince loves. As the Highgrove gardeners explain, "The lawns are green for most of the year and contribute to the overall tapestry of plants which make up a green space. To all intents and purposes, provided they are regularly mown so that there are visible stripes, they appear to be lawns. We've never had adverse comments from visitors. They are as close to Nature as this sort of thing can be and if we stopped mowing, they would quickly become a wildflower meadow, which is what happens just the other side of the yew hedge." Where there is formal structure in the ornamental gardens, for example close to the yew hedges, the edges of the grass are neatly clipped in Summer, but generally they are left alone as Prince Charles prefers to see the borders and lawns meeting in a natural way.

The classic green sward, kept trimmed within an inch of its life and with not a weed in sight, does not fit comfortably into an organically managed garden. It is a form of monoculture (growing one type of plant and excluding all others), bringing with it all the problems this entails. Monoculture is an unnatural state, where plants require extra management because pests and diseases spread readily in the homogenous environment. A more relaxed approach is less labour intensive and more environmentally friendly, both in terms of doing away with all the weedkillers and fertilizers that are habitually spread on lawns, and in cutting down on water usage.

*"A mossy lawn is a beautiful thing in its own right."*

HRH THE PRINCE OF WALES

*Instead of conventional lawns, Highgrove has species-rich green spaces which are mown regularly to give the appearance of lawns. These are far less labour intensive and more environmentally friendly.*

# The gardens

THE TERRACE GARDEN on the West side of the house was one of the first areas to be developed by Prince Charles. He created it as a place close to the house where he could sit surrounded by his favourite scented plants. The two pavilions at the outer corners, together with the central octagonal pool, were designed by William Bertram. Inside each pavilion there is room for a single seat. Set into the wall behind each of them there is a panel of tiles designed by Prince Charles, who drew inspiration from the many plants that grow on the terrace, especially his particular favourite, the Mexican orange blossom (*Choisya*).

This area was planned to be as natural as possible. The plants are allowed to spread and self-seed with only a minimum of control. Much of the planting is now mature or even over-mature, but Prince Charles loves it this way and has no plans to change any of it. Although the terrace is dominated by the cedar, none of the plants seem to suffer because its branches are so high above them. Early in the year self-sown primroses and aquilegias emerge from every crack and crevice, followed in Summer by the golden form of lemon balm, *Melissa officinalis* 'Aurea', and *Alchemilla mollis*. In the narrow borders a mix of shrubs and perennials billow out on to the paving and jostle up against the self-sown plants. Brushing against the lemon balm releases its refreshing scent into the air, where it mixes with the fragrance of the other plants.

One of the joys of this relaxed style of garden is that it invites the gardener to sit back and enjoy the surroundings. When every crack in the paving is filled with attractive plants there is less need to get up and weed, although Prince Charles is very clear he does still weed it regularly. However, once the plants are large and well established, they will largely look after themselves and the scent-filled air does encourage one to linger.

The terrace is also home to a large proportion of Prince Charles's collection of terracotta pots from around the world. Some are grouped together on the old steps leading to a disused door, and during the Summer months they contain specimen pelargoniums for added scent and colour. The stone steps that lead to the French windows are flanked by pots of Prince Charles's favourite regal pelargonium, the strongly branched variety 'Rembrandt', which have recently been joined by the 'Marchioness of Bute'. The only weed that creates any problems on the terrace is annual meadow grass and this is removed by hand before it can self-seed.

The Black and White, or Sundial, Garden to the South of the house is planted with a mixture of herbaceous plants and shrubs in a style not used elsewhere at Highgrove. When David was asked by Prince Charles to rework the original garden designed by Lady Salisbury, he devised a garden of strong contrasts where dark and light interplayed in combinations of white against black and black against white.

*One of the yew windows used to display the four bronze busts of Prince Charles can be seen beyond the sundial at the centre of the Black and White Garden.*

*Selections of Prince Charles's favourite plants are allowed to spread and self-seed among the stone slabs of the Terrace Garden. In Spring, the surface is carpeted with primroses, violets, aquilegias and forget-me-nots.*

It was planned as a garden that would be interesting for ten months of the year. In January, the black-stemmed dogwood *Cornus alba* 'Kesselringii' is underplanted with double white snowdrops and the black leaves of *Ophiopogon planiscapus* 'Nigrescens'. In early Spring, white-flowered *Helleborus orientalis* surround the black foliage of *Pittosporum tenuifolium* 'Tom Thumb', followed in early May by a thousand black and white tulips. Once the tulips are finished they are replaced by Summer bedding in shades of black and white. These include *Salvia discolor*, scabious 'Ace of Spades', nemophila 'Penny Black', cosmos 'Purity', *Argyranthemum gracile* 'Chelsea Girl', *Nicotiana sylvestris* 'Only the Lonely' and dahlia 'Bishop of Llandaff', which is grown here purely for its foliage effect (the flowers are picked off). The more sun this dahlia gets, the darker its leaf colour. Contrasts wax and wane through the year until finally the dark-leaved aster 'Lady in Black' is smothered with tiny white star-shaped flowers.

Each year the antique pots in the Black and White Garden feature a different planting scheme. The silver-grey *Salvia discolor* and purple-leaved geranium 'Midnight Reiter' created a wonderful foliage contrast (aided by the removal of

*The Black and White Garden in its Spring finery.*
*Set against a backdrop of immaculately trimmed*
*yew hedges, the colour-themed planting emerges*
*from a sea of green provided by the box hedging*
*and topiary.*

the blue flowers), as did the dramatic blackish-purple rosettes of *Aeonium urbicum* 'Zwartkop' when teamed with the delicate ferny foliage and white daisies of *Argyranthemum gracile* 'Chelsea Girl'. During the Winter, these pots feature clipped box topiary which is replaced by bulbs in early Spring.

The secret of this garden's success is that although its formality dictates that the planting should be symmetrical, it has been recognized that Nature will intervene, so a planting style described as "dissipating symmetry" has been adopted instead. The beds closest to the house have a formal symmetry while those farthest away use the same plants but in less-fixed positions. The great advantage of this is that if a plant fails and has to be replaced it doesn't upset the overall symmetry.

Even in this formal garden the approach is as close to Nature as possible. It is designed around the natural flowering period of the plants and an understanding of how their shape, height and form combine, and can be manipulated, for maximum interest. Even the early removal of the geranium and dahlia flowers is merely a replacement for the more usual dead-heading.

At the far end of the Thyme Walk, the Lily Pool Garden is a favoured spot where the sun shines for most of the day. This is ideal for growing sun-loving plants that cannot be grown elsewhere in the garden, but it is currently being redesigned and it will be a while before the plans are finalized.

The Cottage Garden was devised by Prince Charles with Rosemary Verey. The remit was to make a traditional cottage garden with colour throughout the year, using mixed plantings of trees, shrubs, perennials and a few annuals. Every gardener has favourite plants; for Prince Charles the star of this garden is a peony with a well-nigh unpronounceable name, *Paeonia mlokosewitschii*. More generally referred to as 'Molly the Witch', it has beautifully lobed Spring foliage in a delicate greeny-pink shade, followed a little later by the subtle beauty of its bowl-shaped, primrose-yellow flowers. There is a gentle succession of flowering plants in the Cottage Garden, beginning with masses of naturalized daffodils early in the year. These are mostly tried and tested varieties including 'Empress of Ireland', 'Spellbinder', 'Ice Follies', 'Jenny' and 'Thalia' as well as the exotic 'Chanterelle' and 'Cassata', which are both varieties known as "orchid-flowered" because their corollas (trumpets) are split, giving them flat faces. As they come into bloom they are accompanied by the soft-shaded reticulata iris 'Katherine Hodgkin' and later by yellow crown imperials, *Fritillaria imperialis*. As one flower fades, another takes its place. Blooming in a sea of self-sown forget-me-nots, the pale yellow tulip 'Sweetheart' follows the daffodils.

A little later, one of the highlights of the garden is the striking combination of the lime-green and yellow *Smyrnium perfoliatum* with the orange of *Euphorbia griffithii* 'Fireglow'. Later still, clusters of the drooping pink and green flowers of the Summer bulb *Nectaroscordum siculum* rise above the borders on their long

stems. *Crambe cordifolia* is another Summer favourite; its interesting architectural presence in the garden guarantees it becomes a focal point when it is in flower. Shrubs and trees provide important structure and in some cases evergreen colour too. Despite the trauma of having its top blown out in 1999, a pink-flowered magnolia 'Leonard Messel' has responded by growing much faster and, with its stems reduced to five, it is once again a handsome tree that makes an important contribution to the Spring garden.

The adjacent New Cottage Garden is an area for growing more exotic plants, such as the glossy-leaved Japanese privet, *Ligustrum japonicum* 'Rotundifolium', an extraordinarily slow-growing evergreen shrub which reaches only 4 feet in height after 30 years. Its deciduous neighbour, the Japanese angelica tree *Aralia elata*, with its spiny stems and pinnate leaves (borne either side of a central stem), has no trouble growing to a very handsome 30 feet, although here it will be pruned to keep it no higher than 10 feet. Arum lilies, *Zantedeschia aethiopica*, have proved

*The formality of the yew hedges in the Cottage Garden is softened by the gentle curves of the planting in the borders. The limited palette pulls the different elements together and prevents the garden looking cluttered.*

to be surprisingly hardy in the borders and flower well in early Summer, followed later by the vibrant colour of herbaceous lobelias 'Russian Princess' and *L.* x. *gerardii* 'Vedrariensis'.

Throughout the year there is a steady programme of maintenance in the borders to avoid a seasonal peak of work. From January to March the herbaceous plants are cut back, the borders are lightly forked, weeded and mulched and the plant supports are put in place. The large ones are made *in situ* while the smaller ones are constructed in the yard and then moved into place. Dead-heading and cutting back plants after they have flowered keeps the borders tidy and extends the flowering season of many plants.

The Carpet Garden, inspired by the rich colours and symmetrical design of two Turkish carpets at Highgrove House, was originally conceived for the 2001 Chelsea Flower Show, where it won a silver-gilt medal. Its design was a collaboration between Prince Charles, Mike Miller, then Director of Clifton Gardens, and Emma Clark from the Prince's School of Traditional Arts. After the show, the garden was rebuilt alongside the Orchard Room, concealed behind a high wall. Emma Clark says of the garden, "Peace, *Salaam*, is the only word uttered in the Islamic gardens of Paradise as portrayed in the Qur'an. The Carpet Garden is, in essence, a reflection of these gardens, a sanctuary from the outside world whose beauty, calm and sound of water conspire to incline the soul of the visitor towards a profound and heartfelt peace."

The external walls of the Carpet Garden are built from render and Cotswold stone; it is only when you pass through its gates that you are transported to a hidden Islamic garden. Had the external walls been given the same finish as the

ABOVE: *The fountain at the centre of the Carpet Garden, viewed through the open doors. When these doors are closed, the stone and render external walls of the Carpet Garden give no hint of the exotic interior.*

RIGHT: *Inside the Carpet Garden another door is decorated in Moorish style with studded timbers and painted patterns. Wisterias frame the doorway – within the enclosed space of this garden their scent is even more intense.*

interior it would have looked out of place. As it is, the exterior is entirely appropriate and the interior is a delightful discovery.

There is a long history of experimenting with design and planting in English gardens and the Carpet Garden continues this fine tradition. The challenges were considerable, both in terms of finding plants and materials to evoke an Eastern garden while surviving the rigours of the English climate, and that were sympathetic to one another and to their surroundings. Some adaptations have been made: pastel colours are softer to work with against the generally paler sky in this country with its more diffuse Northern light; the external walls use local materials to incorporate the garden harmoniously in its setting; and some of the tender exotics have been replaced by hardier plants to make it more sustainable in our climate. All of these factors are important considerations when a gardener

RIGHT: *The marble bowl, with its gently bubbling fountain and mosaic tile surround, is the centrepiece of the Carpet Garden. The garden is designed to awaken the senses with its vibrant colours, varied textures, soft sounds and clouds of fragrance.*

BELOW: *Despite the exotic appearance of the Carpet Garden, most of the planting is hardy, with only the potted plants needing Winter protection. It is important to Prince Charles that each of the Highgrove gardens is as sustainable as possible.*

wishes to introduce a garden style that is alien to the locality. Most importantly, there should be a separation from the wider landscape or it can look odd or even ridiculous. This doesn't apply exclusively to gardens from distant lands; a seaside-style garden deep in the country or halfway up a mountain simply looks perverse unless there is an element of concealment. The wilder shores of garden experimentation work best in an urban environment, where there is complete separation from the landscape.

The Carpet Garden is closed down during the Winter months. The citrus and other tender trees are moved to the greenhouses and the central marble bowl is drained, and together with its mosaic surroundings, is covered with 30 bales of straw and three large tarpaulins. None of this is apparent from outside, where the enclosing stone wall offers protection and a sense of secrecy.

# Features of the gardens

WATER IS IMPORTANT in a garden. As well as attracting birds and insects, it encourages the gardener to pause and reflect. It embodies both meanings of the word "reflection", mirroring the sky above and inviting a pause for thought. Organic gardening is about the quality of life of everything within the garden and this includes the gardener.

The water features in these gardens are architectural and are intended as focal points or places of quiet reverie, rather than somewhere to grow aquatic and marginal plants. On the terrace between the house and the Thyme Walk there is an octagonal pool where water quietly bubbles up through the central circular stone and flows over its surface into a pebble-filled pool. At the far end of the Thyme Walk, the Lily Pool Garden features a quatrefoil pool designed by local architect Willy Bertram. It contains a cruciform water feature made by William Pye in which waters gently flow from four identical waterspouts to the pool below. In the Carpet Garden a water-filled, marble bowl bubbles gently at the heart of this Eastern-inspired enclosed space. The high walls shut out the surroundings and draw the eye towards the bowl at its centre.

Throughout the gardens, in keeping with the philosophy behind the design, all the paths and paving are made of natural materials from local sustainable or salvaged sources. They vary from classic flagstones to less formal mixtures of stone, brick and cobble, hard-wearing and practical gravel or hoggin, or, at their simplest, grass paths which curve round borders or are mown through meadows.

When Prince Charles embarked on redesigning the formal gardens, the Thyme Walk was a personal project. He replaced the gravel path that ran between the golden yews with a mixed paving of flagstones, granite and bricks, all inter-planted with different species of thyme. Before he began, he sought the advice of the late Rosemary Verey and Sir Roy Strong, both of whom advised against this and argued in favour of removing the golden yews. Despite his high regard for their opinions, he ignored them completely and spent every available weekend over the following three months personally planting the thymes.

For a number of years the Thyme Walk was highly successful; however, the soil type is quite heavy with a clay subsoil and it attracted perennial weeds, creating problems in its care and management. To improve this situation, the top soil was removed, complete with thyme and weeds, and 15 tons of pea gravel dug in to improve the drainage. The entire area was then covered with a woven polypropylene membrane to suppress the perennial weeds and conserve moisture. Holes were cut in this and new thyme plants were planted into the soil with a further 20 tons of gravel added as a mulch. This created the perfect conditions for the thymes: it was effectively a horizontal mountain scree, easy to manage, no weeds, no watering, and it has cut down on maintenance by 80 per

ABOVE: *As in the Carpet Garden, there are only the softest of sounds from the octagonal pool in the Terrace Garden. Gently bubbling water is restful and conducive to thought; hectic movement is energizing and stimulating.*

RIGHT: *The imperceptible movement of water over the rim of one of the waterspouts in the quatrefoil pool in the Lily Garden doesn't disturb the perfect reflection of the house and the cedar of Lebanon.*

*"It is to achieve a sense of harmony that I have, over the past 26 years, worked with various people whose professional skills I admire in order to blend the arts of the imagination and architecture into what, I hope, has gradually become a garden which delights the eye, warms the heart and feeds the soul."*

HRH THE PRINCE OF WALES

cent. All that is necessary is for the thymes to be cut back after flowering and tidied in the Spring. A recent addition to the planting is Corsican mint, *Mentha requienii*, a creeping mint with a piercing and invigorating fragrance which is released when the plants are walked upon.

In gardening, as in evolution, it is sometimes a case of "adapt or die". If the conditions in the garden are not suited to the plant, the gardener must find a way of adapting them. This will always be more work than growing plants that are

naturally suited to the soil, but sometimes, as in the Thyme Walk, the gardener considers the effort worthwhile. (For more information on how to grow thyme successfully see The Blueprint, page 163.)

Over the past few years a material called hoggin has been adopted as the favoured material for the most heavily used paths in the garden. Hoggin varies in different parts of the country, making it an ideal and sympathetic local material. Sometimes it is a mix of shale and clay, other times flint and clay; at Highgrove it is bought as as "dug gravel", which contains every soil particle size from clay, through silt and sand to gravel that can be as large as flints of 1½ inches in diameter. Laid on a prepared surface (usually granite scalpings or hardcore) and rolled, it gives a hard, durable surface, which is natural in origin and appearance, and inexpensive to install. In time, it is softened by moss growing at the edges and occasionally, but not frequently enough to be a problem, a plant will set up home. Compared with flagstones it has the advantage of not being slippery, and it copes well with the 25,000 pairs of feet that walk on it each year.

The beds and borders at Highgrove are both an inspiration and a reassurance. Inspiring because there are wonderful planting combinations to emulate, and reassuring because they are full of lush, healthy plants which clearly thrive in the organic environment. There is nothing scruffy or dull here and very little sign of any insect, slug or snail damage. A well-managed organic ornamental garden should be indistinguishable from one that is conventionally managed, except perhaps for the absence of the blue slug pellets that seem so ubiquitous in many

*The Thyme Walk has recently been replanted, following work to reduce maintenance and make the soil more thyme-friendly. The conditions are now near perfect and the thymes need nothing more than cutting back after flowering and tidying in Spring.*

gardens. By avoiding the use of such chemical controls the garden becomes more attractive to wildlife, which will control, but not eliminate, the pests that damage the plants. This establishes an equilibrium that helps support the natural food chain within the garden.

There is no rose garden at Highgrove, to avoid creating a monoculture with all the attendant pest and disease problems. When grown in the borders among other plants, roses are far less problematic than they are in a dedicated rose garden. Provided they are given 3 square feet of clear soil around them while they establish themselves, roses are perfectly happy in mixed planting.

There is a wide range of roses at Highgrove, particularly gallicas, rugosas, hybrid teas and David Austin English Roses (see The Blueprint, page 163 for contact details). There are also some damasks, bourbons and centifolias and generally there is little problem with disease except for a climbing rose called 'Leverkusen' which suffers terribly from black spot and defoliates each year. It is marked for removal when it no longer performs a part as a useful ornamental climber, but in the meantime all the affected leaves are picked up and burnt to avoid black spot spreading elsewhere.

Today's rose breeders are far more aware of the need to breed roses with plenty of natural vigour and good disease resistance. They know that it is now possible to find modern, healthy alternatives to the old, weak varieties with all their inherent problems. Modern varieties have all the charm and fragrance of their forebears but none of their drawbacks.

# Ornamentation

Beyond the usual considerations of climate, location and function, other factors influence the appearance of a garden, including taste, fashion and circumstance. While most of us are unlikely to have more than one or two statues in our gardens, Prince Charles has a huge number of works of art, from the classical statuary on the main lawn to contemporary slate pots on the edge of the Wildflower Meadow. He likes to find suitable places for these that he feels enhance the gardens and act as "eye-catchers". Some were gifts and others were commissioned by the Prince, including many bronze or stone busts of people he admires such as Sir John Tavener, Dame Miriam Rothschild, Dr Kathleen Raine, Sir Laurens van der Post, Ted Hughes, Dr Vandana Shiva and the Dowager Duchess of Devonshire.

*This bust of the Dowager Duchess of Devonshire by Angela Connors was given to Prince Charles by the sculptress for his "Wall of Worthies" in the Azalea Walk. The Prince spends considerable time positioning each of the works of art in the garden.*

*This yew is being topiarized within metal frames to represent Platonic and Archimedean Solids. The shapes are rich in mathematical significance and philosophical meaning.*

*"The inscription above the entrance to the Arboretum reads 'The garden is a reflection of the stars of the sky'. Similarly, the garden is a reflection of the gardener and develops around a series of ideas and decisions that he or she makes."*

HRH THE PRINCE OF WALES

Careful thought is given to the works of art and where they are placed within the gardens. Sometimes Prince Charles will know instinctively, while at other times the positioning of a sculpture requires more thought and will take longer while he considers which site will be most appropriate and allow the piece to have most impact. Such things may need to be considered in any garden, especially when the object involved is difficult to manoeuvre. You will quickly run out of willing helpers if you keep changing your mind about where the item should go. One way to avoid this situation is to find something of similar dimensions and outline, for example, a stepladder or a dustbin, and try it in a variety of positions. By viewing it from all angles you will be able to gauge the effect your sculpture or statue will have on the garden.

There are hidden details too, which reveal that the garden is a place where Prince Charles considers the deeper questions of life. Platonic (and a selection of Archimedean) Solids are replicated in topiarized yew. These Solids are symmetrical mathematical shapes in which all sides are equal, all angles are the same and all faces are identical. In Ancient Greece the Solids represented the elements: earth, water, fire, air and a fifth element, the universe, which was represented by the 12-sided solid, the dodecahedron. The yew bushes, trained within metal frames, symbolize forms that Plato called "ever-true" and what is referred to as "solid state" in modern physics. (See The Blueprint, page 163 for fuller descriptions of Platonic and Archimedean Solids.)

At the central point along the Thyme Walk the seats have small three-dimensional carvings of four of the Solids, while the fifth, the dodecahedron, is

*These beautifully ornate bird feeders hang beneath the cedar of Lebanon in the Terrace Garden. They are much visited by the local bird population which helps to control insect pests.*

buried at the axis of the paths with only one facet visible. This is a symbolic reflection of the universe. As above, so below.

Close examination reveals that there is also a distinct air of fun in this very personal garden. The bench concealed within one of the temples in the Stumpery Garden is home to a pair of whimsical Irish leprechauns fashioned from clay; a present from a friend in Ireland. Closer to the house, dangling beneath the branches of the cedar tree, there are four beautifully detailed bird feeders in ornate oriental shapes. Whether the constant stream of visiting birds appreciates the finer architectural details of the three miniature pagodas and the Thai Temple hanging bird basket is questionable, but this fine blend of beauty and utility has turned something rather mundane into a collective work of art. Similarly, the gothic-style Chicken House, created by folly-maker Richard Craven, has more than a touch of Hansel and Gretel about it. Surrounded by a rustic cleft-paling fence, it demonstrates that a chicken house needn't be a boring shed with a felt roof. And even if it is, it can be greatly enhanced by customizing it with a shingle or tile roof, a coat of paint and attractive fencing.

Ornament doesn't necessarily last indefinitely. Like the garden itself it evolves and changes over time, sometimes through wear and tear and sometimes through changing taste. In the Walled Garden a new arbour has recently replaced an earlier one that was made 20 years ago. When the tree supporting the Tree House in the Stumpery Garden died, the structure was repositioned on a supporting platform designed by Stephen Florence. The platform rests on slate uprights and additional upright slate stones were incorporated into the surroundings, giving this area a different feel to the rest of the Stumpery Garden.

At Highgrove, focal points designed to draw the eye in a particular direction have been incorporated as the garden has developed. The first was the Dovecote, which is situated at the far end of a tree-lined walk and visible from the West door of the house. In front of the Main Entrance, another walk leads to the golden bird which perches on a nest at the top of an iron column that was once part of Victoria railway station. This same focal point is shared with a newly planted avenue of 40 Princeton American elms leading from the rear of the Orchard Room towards the golden bird. A wedding present, these trees are resistant to Dutch elm disease and have allowed the reintroduction of elms to the Highgrove Estate.

Walls and buildings throughout the garden are built primarily from Cotswold stone. This is the local stone and using it allows the garden to sit comfortably in the wider landscape. In contrast to its layered, silvery-grey appearance, monumental pieces of redundant and recycled cathedral stone have been incorporated in several places to add drama and age to the garden. The sensitive use of natural, local, hard-landscaping materials is the key to giving a garden a sense of place and is environmentally sound.

*The Dovecote stands at the far end of the vista that leads from the House, passes along the Thyme Walk, over the Lily Pool and down the avenue of limes. It helps to draw the eye beyond the garden.*

Prince Charles has commissioned local craftsmen to make a variety of seating for the garden, using sustainable materials. This bench, in the Terrace Garden, has been made from Dorset Ham stone and Highgrove oak.

Although the painted benches in the garden are very eye-catching, they have proved to need a great deal of maintenance to look their best. More recent commissions use hardwoods that can be left unpainted and will weather naturally.

There is little point in creating a delightful garden with glorious plants, secret corners and wonderful vistas unless you also create places where you can sit down and appreciate it all. Highgrove is rich in such places and each of the seats is an artwork in its own right. Over the years, Prince Charles has commissioned talented craftsmen to make a variety of seating using sustainable materials such as English oak and FSC (Forest Stewardship Council) approved teak. The seats are variously positioned for the view, privacy, shelter, sun in Spring and Autumn, or shade in Summer, and also for the benefit of elderly visitors when the Prince realized they needed somewhere to rest as they went round the garden. Five of

*This Chinese Chippendale style seat stands in the Cottage Garden. It has a central plaque that is embellished with the Prince of Wales feathers.*

*One of a pair of delicately wrought seats which stand against the hedges either side of the Black and White Garden. The white paintwork stands out against the dark backdrop of the yew and was a natural choice for this colour-themed garden.*

the original softwood benches survive, all painted in bright colours, but more recent examples use materials that weather well and need not be painted. Behind the Orchard Room stands a rather firm stone sofa, while in the Woodland Garden there is an inviting tub chair carved from the base of a dead beech tree. Using Dorset Ham stone and Highgrove oak, Stephen Florence fashioned the bench around the cedar tree in the Terrace Garden, as well as a simple horseshoe-shaped bench constructed from Hereford oak and Welsh granite around the sculpture, *The Daughters of Odessa*, in the Arboretum. More conventionally, fine antique stone seats are set into alcoves in the yew hedges that flank the main lawn.

It can be difficult to sit down in a garden and simply enjoy your surroundings. All too often the eye falls on something that needs doing and before you are even aware of what is happening you will be on your knees attending to it. There can be a perception that organic gardening is all about toil at the expense of pleasure; ideally it should be a blend of the two. A good way to balance the work/enjoyment ratio of a garden is to take breakfast or tea outside, or enjoy an evening stroll with a glass of wine rather than a pair of secateurs.

Pots are another important decorative element in the Highgrove gardens, creating focal points, punctuation marks and ornamental flourishes. Prince Charles has a collection of terracotta pots from around the world, of which approximately half are displayed as objects of beauty in their own right, with no additional embellishment. When used in this way garden pots make a simple architectural statement that can be as effective as a piece of sculpture.

The rest of the pots in his collection are planted up each year using a technique that has been devised to protect the terracotta from damage. Plants are potted into a plastic pot with a diameter marginally smaller than the neck of the

*Pots do not need to be planted to look beautiful. Here, some of Prince Charles's terracotta pots from around the world are displayed as sculptural objects on steps leading up to the House from the Terrace Garden.*

terracotta pot. This is lowered inside the terracotta pot and rests on a bed of woodchip that fills the remaining space. Using this method, the soil remains cool and moist but any excess water drains through, while the airspaces in the woodchip ensure that the pot will not crack in frosty weather. This is a useful technique, particularly for narrow-necked pots which it can sometimes be necessary to break in order to remove a plant that has developed a large rootball. It also reduces the amount of watering that is needed; in clay pots water migrates from the soil to the terracotta and is lost through evaporation, but in plastic pots the moisture is retained. One note of caution: the moist woodchip will be very attractive to slugs and snails – it is a good idea to lift out the inner pot from time to time and remove any that you may find lurking there.

Plastic pots are widely used behind the scenes at Highgrove. David explains: "There is a common misconception that becoming organic involves stepping back a hundred years and that we should only be using clay pots. If we did this we would need an army of gardeners because they dry out in no time. From a practical point of view I advocate using plastic pots. We use them over and over again and when pots finally split they are taken to the local recycling centre where they are chipped and recycled. In the eight years I have been here we have only bought additional pots on one occasion, when they were needed for the plants sold in the shop. As for the rest, on wet or frosty days the gardeners wash them in soapy water ready for the next time they are needed. As a concession to the 21st century this traditional task is now done in warm water!" He has looked at organic alternatives to plastic such as miscanthus (a grass), vegetable oil and even feathers and will consider their use once the garden's stock of plastic pots runs low.

*To create a balanced and attractive Summer display in a large pot, the chosen plants – still in their plastic pots – are arranged on the soil surface. Only when the required effect is achieved, will they be knocked out of their pots and planted directly into the soil.*

# Maintenance

As in the Productive Garden, natural materials, mainly sourced from the estate, are used as plant supports throughout the Ornamental Gardens. Large woven-willow and hazel tepees are made *in situ* by the gardeners, while coppiced hazel pea sticks and woven-willow give plants discreet support in the herbaceous borders. These are put in position in early Spring to allow the plants to grow through them and quickly render them nearly invisible.

There are few problems with pests and disease control in the Ornamental Gardens. Natural predators are the primary pest controllers. A thriving population of birds and beneficial insects amply repays the provision of suitable habitats by dealing with the vast majority of pests. There is also a certain amount of hand-picking by the gardeners who are always on the lookout for a developing problem. This may be all that is needed, but in the event of a serious infestation, they will spray with Eradicoat, a starch-based organic insecticide.

Careful selection of disease-resistant varieties and a soil kept healthy by an annual top-dressing of compost generally keeps diseases at bay. Where problems do occur, infected material is removed and burned.

The three ornamental greenhouses are tucked away in a sheltered yard next to the Apple Store. During the Winter months they are used primarily to house a forest of tender plants. These include the citrus and pomegranate trees which spend the Summer months in the Carpet Garden, along with the many plants that form Summer displays in pots around the gardens. The smallest of the greenhouses also doubles as a propagation house where all the seed sowing and pricking out of seedlings takes place. Jess Usher keeps a watchful eye on everything and deals with any of the pests that can be a problem in greenhouses. She keeps the air moist by damping down (watering) the paths to deter the red spider mite – it thrives in a dry atmosphere – and by introducing natural predators such as *Encarsia formosa*, which are tiny parasitic wasps that control whitefly. This is another example of working with Nature; as soon as an infestation is noticed, Jess introduces the predator that will feed on it and keep it under control. (See The Blueprint, pages 161–62 for a list of pests and their predators.)

The greenhouses also supply foliage and flowering plants to the House, for events and to decorate the Orchard Room throughout the year. Florist, Sarah Champier, looks after them, bringing them on, arranging the displays indoors when they are at their peak and returning them to the greenhouse to rest and recuperate after their moment of glory. There is a wide range of plants from tiny African violets to tall palms, with clivias, azaleas and gardenias in between. Suspended above the other plants are the air-feeding Vanda orchids. These are great favourites of Prince Charles. Their care involves a daily spraying of their long dangling roots with water until they turn from near-white to green.

ABOVE: *The natural plant supports, made from hazel and willow grown at Highgrove, are easy to construct, subtle and effective. At the end of the season they can be shredded and used as a mulch on paths or under trees.*

RIGHT: *The attractive hazel and willow tepees, which add height to the borders, are all made by the Highgrove gardeners. This skill can be learnt at one of the many willow-weaving courses held throughout the country.*

4

The Informal Gardens

*"At 25 years of age this is a relatively young meadow and it will take many more years of continuous and sustainable management – of grazing and cutting for hay – to create the rich tapestry of plants that our forefathers knew. I have learnt that our natural heritage is a fragile thing and we should handle it with great care."*

HRH THE PRINCE OF WALES

# The Wildflower Meadow

PRINCE CHARLES SAYS of this area, "It was with my dear friend Dame Miriam Rothschild that I first explored the reintroduction of wild flowers into the meadows at Highgrove. Appalled by the destruction wreaked during the 1960s and '70s, which led to a total disregard for the most humble aspects of Nature – for wildlife and the countryside – I was eager to make changes. The first part to be altered was the meadow (parkland) on the Southern side of the house. Its development over the last 25 years has encouraged me to establish more meadows and sustainable management systems across the entire estate.

"At 25 years of age this is a relatively young meadow and it will take many more years of continuous and sustainable management – of grazing and cutting for hay – to create the rich tapestry of plants that our forefathers knew. I have learnt that our natural heritage is a fragile thing and we should handle it with great care. What has taken hundreds, if not thousands, of years to develop through a gentle combination of Man and Nature can be destroyed by modern machinery in a morning. But have we got enough patience, or understanding, or sympathy or long-term vision to ensure that our descendants can enjoy things of untold beauty? Beauty is what the human soul aspires to and responds to. And yet we persist in creating ugliness all around us with no thought for the future."

Today, wildflower meadows are fashionable and roadside verges are valued as essential refuges for flora and fauna, but 26 years ago attitudes were very different. If you had walked through the parkland at Highgrove you would not have seen any wild flowers. All the "nasty weeds" had been killed off by herbicides and replaced by a grass monoculture that allowed no interlopers.

Prince Charles was an early pioneer of the reintroduction of wildflower habitats. With the help of the late Dame Miriam Rothschild, an early and passionate advocate of biodiversity, he set about the development of the meadow

*In Spring the meadow is a mass of naturalized daffodils. They fit in well with the cycle of management of this area, which will not be mown until long after the daffodil foliage has died back.*

*Fastigiate (upright) hornbeams line the path that leads from the formal gardens surrounding the House to the informal gardens on the far side of the Wildflower Meadow. The trees guard the path and discourage visitors from wandering into the meadow.*

at Highgrove. Miriam Rothschild devised a seed mix to replicate the old meadows that had been lost, using 120 different species that were typical of the natural flora of Gloucestershire. The seed was slot-seeded (a technique that cuts a groove in turf and drops seeds at intervals) directly into the sward using an ordinary agricultural drill. For some years you would never have known that anything had been sown, but eventually the wild flowers established themselves and started to spread. Growth was variable – lush in the moisture-retentive clay soil, more sparse in the free-draining Cotswold brash – but as the fertility fell the wild flowers increasingly took over from the grasses. And, as Miriam Rothschild had predicted, the yellow rattle in her seed mixture helped suppress the coarse grasses in the meadow. While most plants benefit from improved soil fertility, the reverse is true for wild flowers.

The meadow is managed as a traditional hay field. These meadows are man-made systems that don't occur naturally and are the result of a specific management regime. The best way to improve a meadow is to stick to the same

*This colourful mixture of cornfield annuals lining the main drive is known as 'Farmer's Nightmare' because it contains plants not generally welcomed by modern farmers – poppies, corncockle, cornflowers and cornfield marigolds.*

*Black Hebridean sheep graze the meadow from August to October. The aim is to remove virtually all the grass and trample the surface so that the wildflower seeds are incorporated into the soil, ready to germinate in March.*

regime year after year. By cutting and removing the biomass (hay/silage) during the Summer and grazing it in Winter, the wild flowers have gradually increased as a direct result of these actions.

The basic programme at Highgrove is to cut the meadows when the optimum cutting, drying and baling conditions occur; this is usually in July. Hay is made if the sun shines enough to dry the crop, silage if it doesn't. The cutting is done mainly by farm machinery due to time constraints, although Suffolk Punch horses are used to cut the difficult bits of the meadow. However, as hedge cutting begins immediately after haymaking, time is always in short supply. Even with machinery, this is not a system for the faint-hearted and does involve a huge amount of work.

The timing pays no heed to the flowering period of plants in the meadow and has a big effect on the species present, which will vary from year to year. It is essential to remove the biomass to prevent its inherent fertility returning to the meadow. By repeating this annually, a low-fertility system is created where wild flowers take over, grasses are reduced, and a natural balance is established. This balance is maintained by further removals of the biomass during the Summer. Traditionally this would have been done by grazing the meadow with cattle or

sheep and at Highgrove the aim is to try and graze with sheep during the months of August, September and October, since the sooner the meadow is grazed after cutting the better.

Electric fences are erected around the areas to be grazed and guards fixed round the trees to prevent damage. The availability of sheep from Home Farm dictates the numbers (it could be anything from 25 rams to 250 ewes), but however many there are, the sheep are left to graze on the meadow until they have removed all of the grass. Any breed of sheep can be used, but the rare breed of Black Hebridean is favoured here at Highgrove because it will eat absolutely anything. The animals leave behind them a very muddy field with virtually no grass. Their feet disturb the ground, treading in the seeds which will start germinating in March, giving the resultant seedlings the maximum chance to grow and get away before the grass starts growing. No further management of the meadows is necessary from March until July.

Healthy populations of locally occurring wild flowers have now managed to re-establish themselves in the Highgrove meadow. Wild daffodils, *Narcissus pseudonarcissus*, grow in an area that appears on old maps as 'Daffodil', while snakeshead fritillaries, *Fritillaria meleagris*, have been reintroduced and three species of orchid – Marsh, Southern and Early Purple orchids – have appeared on the lower, damp side of the meadow. The numbers are small at present; they have taken a long time to return, but have done so of their own accord and have not been introduced. What can be destroyed in an afternoon with modern

*The meadow shortly before it is cut in July. By removing the crop and using it for hay or silage the fertility of the meadow is kept low, creating optimum conditions for the wild flowers.*

*The snakeshead fritillary is a native plant in the Cotswolds and has been successfully reintroduced to the damper areas of the Wildflower Meadow. It is now being planted either side of the main path as a sustainable alternative to tulips.*

machinery takes hundreds of years of continuous and sensitive management to bring back. Sometimes hay from existing wildflower-rich meadows can be used to spread on a field after cutting in the hope that some seed will be gradually transferred elsewhere.

Two strips of cornfield annuals line the main driveway. These originate from Miriam Rothschild's special seed mix 'Farmer's Nightmare'; so called because it contains plants that most modern farmers do not want among their corn – these include poppies, pink corncockle, cornflowers and cornfield marigolds. These differ from the meadow flowers and are what are described by botanists as "ephemeral" and by gardeners as "short-lived annuals", growing and seeding themselves in three to five months. This is their complete lifecycle, but when flowering is over they leave behind sufficient seed for future generations. In September, once the plants have seeded, the verges are mown and the biomass is composted. The only other requirement is freshly disturbed soil which is provided by rotavating the top couple of inches of soil in early Spring. Provided the seed is allowed to fall and the ground is cultivated at the right time, cornfield annuals will return year after year.

In establishing both these meadows Prince Charles has paid special attention to the seed, taking care that it consists of varieties local to the Gloucestershire and Wiltshire area. Naturally occurring species can vary from one geographical area to another and over a long period will develop into unique subspecies or varieties that have been influenced by many factors, not just the locality. The Prince liaises with the Wiltshire Wildlife Trust who regularly measure species numbers at Highgrove.

For advice on establishing a wildflower meadow, make contact with your local Wildlife Trust. They are the best people to advise on a particular locality; sites vary enormously and local knowledge is essential. Find out contact details by going to their website (www.wildlifetrusts.org) and then key in your postcode to find a local branch. For a comprehensive list of your local flora, refer to the Natural History Museum's Postcode Plants Database on their website (www.nhm.ac.uk). Based on the third edition of the *Atlas of the British Flora*, this lists every plant that is native to an area, but does include historic plants that may no longer exist locally.

There are many seed companies offering exciting ranges of wildflower seeds, but these don't always state the country of origin. There is a risk that imported seed may contain alien species that could become invasive. One need only consider the problems caused by Japanese knotweed, *Fallopia japonica*, and Himalayan balsam, *Impatiens glandulifera*, to realize that introduced plants can prove harmful where there is no natural predator to keep them under control. This is a two-way process; when David was in Ohio he was shown how a British native, garlic mustard, *Alliaria petiolata*, has spread alarmingly and is pushing out local species. However, it should also be borne in mind that many of the plants we enjoy in our gardens are not native to the British Isles and make our gardens more interesting without posing any danger.

There is a good example of this at Highgrove, where Prince Charles has embellished the Wildflower Meadow by planting the North American camassia, or Quamash lily, *Camassia leichtlinii caerulea*, without putting the wild flowers at any risk. Although it is an alien species, the camassia will not spread, colonize or hybridize because the seedhead is cut off with the hay crop long before the seed can ripen. Originally 2,000 bulbs were introduced and there has been an annual planting of 500 ever since, resulting in a glorious tapestry of blue and yellow when their flowering coincides with that of the native buttercup.

Similarly, many years ago, Prince Charles established a Tulip Walk to link the gardens surrounding the House to the Kitchen Gardens. This much-admired feature was created by planting the bulbs directly into the ground each November. Because the tulip is growing outside its natural geography and topography it is unlikely to multiply in a Cotswold meadow. In the wild, it is a high-desert plant which can stand extreme cold, but likes to be dry and cannot stand "wet feet" or competition from other plants. Recently however, a fungal disease known as tulip fire became apparent in the Walk and it was decided to

*A spectacular display of camassias and buttercups is the highlight of the Wildflower Meadow in early Summer. Although camassias are not native, there is no danger of them spreading because the seed heads are cut off long before the seed can ripen.*

take a more sustainable approach by planting native snakeshead fritillaries instead, as they are well-suited to wildflower meadows (see The Blueprint, page 164 for information on how to recognize and deal with tulip fire). The fritillaries will take longer to establish than the Tulip Walk, but represent a permanent and sustainable solution which will continue to link the two garden areas with a ribbon of purple in the Spring. This will be further enhanced by the purple alliums being planted in the same area.

Lining the Tulip Walk is an avenue of fastigiated (upright) hornbeams. They were chosen for both practical and aesthetic reasons. In practical terms, their neat symmetrical habit ensures that they don't cast much shade on the meadow. They were also selected by Prince Charles because he kept noticing the beautiful shape of fastigiated hornbeams when driving along a particular road on the edge of Oxford. It then transpired that these are the very same hornbeams on the same section of road that features in Philip Pullman's trilogy, *His Dark Materials*.

Other ornamental trees that have been planted in this area by Prince Charles are surrounded by circular hedges echoing the shape of the tree's canopy. These will be removed when the trees reach maturity, but in the meantime they add to the aesthetic beauty of the Wildflower Meadow and protect the trees from damage by farm machinery.

*"I would like to think that in hundreds of years' time many of the trees that I have planted in the garden, Arboretum and on the estate will still be living. The Stumpery is not only a happily eccentric and atmospheric part of the garden, it is also a monument to the elegant forms created by trees."*

HRH THE PRINCE OF WALES

# The Woodland Garden and Aboretum

TREES, THE LARGEST LIVING THINGS, and climax vegetation to a biologist, are the old men of the natural world. The Woodland Garden is in one of the most atmospheric settings at Highgrove. It contains many strong architectural statements to engage the attention: The Stumpery, The Temple of Worthies, the Wall of Gifts, the Fern Pyramid, and the Tree House, all of which add drama to the scene. Equally important, though, is the light that filters through the tree canopy, spotlighting plants or illuminating clearings in a way that invites the visitor to pause and examine the details, rather than simply hurry past to the next excitement. It is in that pause that other aspects of this place become apparent – the wind rustling the leaves, the birdsong filling the air and the delicate and subtle refinement of the many shade-loving plants. This layering of drama and refinement gives the Woodland Garden, and any other good garden, its atmosphere.

*In Spring, white narcissi carpet the ground beneath the trees in the Arboretum. They are left to die back naturally and will be followed by an equally lovely haze of native bluebells.*

*One of the pair of green-oak classical temples that face one another across a grassy glade in The Stumpery. Hostas, hellebores and native ferns grow among the interlocking tree roots that surround the glade.*

When Prince Charles arrived at Highgrove, this area was an unremarkable and neglected tangle of undergrowth and fallen trees on the edge of the parkland, where brambles, snowberry and ivy covered the ground beneath a cluster of sycamore trees. Initially, it was cleared of its understorey (shrubs and scrubby growth) and planted with grassy paths and island beds. Since then it has evolved gradually.

Ten years ago, Prince Charles asked garden designers Julian and Isabel Bannerman to create the original Stumpery, which features a pair of green-oak classical temples either side of a grassy clearing. This created a glade where hostas, hellebores and the native ferns *Polystichum* and *Dryopteris* (some of the Prince's favourite plants) could be grown among the interlocking tree roots that surround the clearing. An outer-planting of cherry laurel, *Prunus laurocerasus*, and native butcher's broom, *Ruscus aculeatus*, encircles the hostas, hellebores and ferns. This atmospheric green grove is very different from the rest of the original woodland planting. To gain entry to this glade one must pass through an archway of antler-like sweet chestnut stumps. As with the Carpet Garden, entering the Stumpery is a gradual process of discovery, the impact of which would be greatly lessened if it were not enclosed.

A stumpery is a Victorian idea, created and developed to grow and display fern collections, which were very much in vogue at that time. In the more recent past, when tree stumps and roots were removed from woodland, they were piled up and burnt, but since Prince Charles established his Stumpery they have become increasingly popular as garden features. A shady corner can be enhanced by the

inclusion of a stump or two, adding sculptural shapes and providing planting crevices at several levels.

By the year 2000, the tree canopy in the Woodland Garden had developed to the point where plants were being shaded out and it was becoming increasingly difficult to maintain them and the paths. Managing a woodland garden is an ongoing process. Most plants prefer dappled light, rather than deep shade, and from time to time it may be necessary to raise the tree canopy by removing lower branches or thin out the trees as they mature. (Depending on where you live, local council permission may be needed to carry out this type of work.)

In 2002, nine sycamores that had been damaged by grey squirrels had to be removed from the Woodland Garden, creating extra space and allowing in additional light. Prince Charles took this opportunity to engage the Bannermans to extend the stumpery theme and incorporate a new water feature. The new Stumpery was formed using 200 tons of topsoil (excavated while preparing the Carpet Garden) to shape raised banks around a further 250 tree stumps. This created a habitat similar to the conditions woodland plants favour in the wild.

While the planting scheme of this new area echoes the simplicity of the original, new plants have brought greater diversity to the entire Woodland Garden. A growing collection of large- and giant-leaved hostas has expanded quickly and was granted Full Collection status by the NCCPG (National Council

*"Recently Ted Green, a man passionate about our trees and natural heritage, has enlightened me as to the plight of our 'ancients'."*

HRH THE PRINCE OF WALES

*Removing the lower branches of the trees has admitted more light into the Woodland Garden. This allows a wider range of plants to be grown, including the thriving bog plants fringing the pond with its spectacular centrepiece.*

*Over the years Prince Charles has collected, and been given, many pieces of architectural stone. He devised the Wall of Gifts as an original way of displaying them.*

for the Conservation of Plants and Gardens – see The Blueprint, page 164) in late 2004. Prince Charles is Patron and a great supporter of the NCCPG, as well as of the British Pteridological Society (see The Blueprint, page 164), and supports their work by displaying collections of hostas and ferns to show how they can be used to great effect alongside other woodland plants. Among his fern collection Prince Charles is particularly proud of a tender tree fern, *Cyathea australis*. It has successfully come through four Winters thanks to a protective coat of straw and sacking and the milder microclimate that exists within the Woodland Garden.

Birds play an important role in the Woodland Garden. Together with a healthy population of slow worms, grass snakes and hedgehogs, they feast on the slugs and snails which might otherwise reduce the hostas to lacework. It is only towards the end of the growing season that any damage becomes apparent. By providing habitats that encourage natural predators to take up residence, the gardeners gain welcome assistance with pest control.

With the exception of a few neatly trimmed hollies and box, the feel of the Woodland Garden is predominantly informal. Rampant clematis and roses climb 30 feet into the tree canopies, beneath which there are craggy rocks topped by "hats" of giant *Gunnera manicata* or creeping thymes, depending on their size. There is also an element of resourcefulness and artistic recycling, evidenced by the tree stumps as well as the curving branches which edge the beds and the fragments of stone making up the Wall of Gifts. Whether viewed in its entirety or in its detail this is a garden where dramatic statements and subtle nuances have found a natural balance.

In the 1950s, well before Prince Charles bought Highgrove, a small plantation of larches had been planted to screen the estate from the road. By the early 1990s, when the Prince was considering how to incorporate this area into the garden, many of the larches were mature and ready to be felled. In maturity, larches become increasingly scruffy as the lower branches progressively die back and drop

ABOVE: *The Fern Pyramid is a contemporary interpretation of a Victorian way of displaying ferns. Beneath the ferns there is a pyramid-shaped wire mesh cage. This was filled with a leaf-mould-rich compost and then planted with ferns.*

*"It is in this part of the garden that one really starts to recognize the complex chains and cycles that exist and inter-relate with other life forms. Slugs, snails and beetles are as much a part of the garden as birds and insects, all of them involved in this, the most natural part of the garden."*

HRH THE PRINCE OF WALES

BELOW: *The healthy, undamaged hosta leaves are a tribute to the effectiveness of the organic management of the garden. The many birds, amphibians and hedgehogs keep the slugs and snails under control. Slug pellets are never used.*

off. This is a useful quality when it is used for timber, but not very desirable in a garden. However, rather than clear-fell the entire area, Prince Charles wisely decided to begin an annual programme of selectively removing the larches and then using the clearings this created gradually to establish an arboretum.

This was an intelligent way to deal with what initially appeared to be an eyesore. If all the larches had been removed, the new trees would have been vulnerable to wind, frost and snow, probably have been slower to establish and needed far more maintenance in their early years. It would also have taken at least 20 years for the Arboretum to gain a semblance of maturity. As it is,

LEFT: *In Autumn the Arboretum puts on a spectacular show of colour. The Prince has specifically chosen liquidambars, Japanese maples and the Katsura tree,* Cercidipyllum japonicum, *for this quality.*

the Arboretum is developing in the same way as a natural wood, with the mature trees offering their protection to the young trees growing among them.

This part of the garden sits on the same seam of rich soil as the Walled Garden and nearby Westonbirt Arboretum, so Prince Charles was confident that the trees would thrive. A great admirer of Westonbirt, he asked the curator at the time, John White, to help him make his first selection of trees. This initial collection was chosen specifically for superb Autumn colour. It includes several of the Prince's favourite Japanese maples, as well as the vivid red sweet gum tree, *Liquidambar,* and the Katsura tree, *Cercidiphyllum japonicum,* which has butter-yellow Autumn foliage and a scent of burnt toffee from its fallen leaves. As the Arboretum grew, John White offered general guidance on balancing the numbers of evergreen and flowering trees to benefit the overall effect, but left the choice of species to Prince Charles, who was thoroughly enjoying creating a woodland full of choice rarities.

*Head Gardener David Howard stands in front of the repositioned Tree House. It was initially built in a holly tree, but when that had to be felled it was re-erected on a platform supported by Welsh slate standing stones.*

This is a wide-ranging collection, encompassing the swamp cypress, *Taxodium distichum,* the giant redwood, *Sequoiadendron giganteum,* the National Beech Collection and a selection of large-flowered magnolias that do particularly well in the deep sandy loam of the Arboretum. Smaller trees and shrubs create an understorey, ensuring that once the larger trees are mature there will still be interest at lower levels. *Malus trilobata* and *Sorbus commixta* provide spectacular Autumn colour and there are many dogwoods and viburnums. With a soil pH of 6.5, it has been possible to incorporate rhododendrons into the Arboretum including the much-admired, large-leaved varieties *R. sino-grande, R. macabeanum, R. falconeri* and *R. mallotum.* Anyone planning to plant trees will find *Hilliers' Manual of Trees & Shrubs* invaluable. At the back of the book there is a list of trees suitable for all types of soil and conditions.

*The Sanctuary stands in a clearing at the heart of the Arboretum. It is built entirely from local materials: local stone, Highgrove-made cob bricks and estate-felled timber, and it is topped by Cotswold tiles.*

Woodland flowers grow in the dappled shade. In Spring there is a scattering of primroses and a haze of bluebells. The vast majority of these are the native bluebell *Hyacinthoides non-scripta*, with its pendant flowers dangling beneath gently curved stems. Should any of the larger, more upright Spanish bluebell, *Hyacinthoides hispanica*, be spotted, they are immediately dug up and replanted in a specific area of the Woodland Garden to ensure that they don't hybridize with their wild relatives.

Currently, five or six larch trees are felled annually. It is calculated that there will be only a few selected larch left in 20 years' time, but by then they will have done their job of providing shelter and shade for the young trees, many of which will have reached a substantial size. The felled timber, which is removed by the rare-breed Suffolk Punch horses so as to minimize damage to the area, is then seasoned before a local contractor arrives at Highgrove with his mobile saw mill and cuts it into planks. The wood is used for various projects on the Highgrove Estate; recently it provided timber for a new chicken house and a feed shed. All of the arboricultural work and felling is done during the Winter; in the Summer months the main task is mowing the paths.

At the heart of the Arboretum is The Sanctuary, a sacred place for Prince Charles, who had it built to commemorate the Millennium. Made of blocks formed from Highgrove clay, it is literally "of this place". The base and dressings are made from local stone, the timber is oak and sweet chestnut, and Cotswold tiles cover the roof. Its design, originally conceived by Sacred Geometer, Keith Critchlow, and then developed by Charles Morris, uses harmonic proportions based on Sacred Geometry. These proportions were traditional in ancient architecture and are still used in many Eastern countries.

*"While I am a passionate advocate of the need to protect our native flora, I also enjoy stretching the boundaries of what can be grown at Highgrove. The Southern Hemisphere Garden is my little bit of exotica in Gloucestershire."*

HRH THE PRINCE OF WALES

# The Southern Hemisphere Garden

PRINCE CHARLES FULLY ACKNOWLEDGES the attractions of this kind of gardening. As he says, "Experimenting with the growing of exotic species is a fine British tradition that has resulted in the introduction of many plants that are familiar in our gardens today. Plants as commonplace as lavender, phlox and wallflower have all been introduced to this country."

The Southern Hemisphere Garden was established in 1999 in an undeveloped area, open to the West, but protected on its other three sides by trees and a wall of the Kitchen Garden. The Prince was curious to know whether tree ferns could be grown at Highgrove and was advised that this spot would afford maximum shelter and long hours of sunshine in what can be, at times, a very cold garden.

They have since found that the tree ferns are hardier than they are given credit for, provided water and frost are excluded from the crown and the top 18 inches of the trunk during the Winter months. The rest of the stem is armour-plated and covered with a protective mass of fibrous roots. In late October, the vulnerable area is wrapped in a blanket of straw and hessian, and the crown is packed with straw and topped with a circular plywood hat which is attached to last year's fronds. This ensures that water is shed away from the crown. Summer care is more demanding; in hot weather it is important to water the stems at least once, and sometimes twice, daily to keep them looking lush.

When buying tree ferns it is essential to check that the plants have a valid export licence tag attached to the trunk. In the past there have been illegal imports which threaten their natural habitats through unregulated harvesting and also risk the import of pests and diseases into the United Kingdom.

Generally, with the exception of three banana trees, the rest of the permanent planting in this garden focuses on hardier Southern hemisphere plants, including eucalyptus, cordylines and phormiums, with a few borderline species such as *Astelia chathamica* and *Beschorneria yuccoides*. The latter seems to struggle a bit, but

ABOVE: *During the Summer, the giant leaves of* Gunnera manicata *conceal the ditch that runs along the Northern side of this garden. This dramatically architectural plant likes to grow in ditches or next to streams.*

RIGHT: *Tree ferns, bananas and palms have proved to be surprisingly hardy in this sheltered part of the garden. When growing these plants, choose the warmest corner of your garden and protect them from Winter wetness, which can be far more damaging than the cold.*

has flowered, sending up impressive spikes 7 feet tall. The seasonal addition of half-hardy cannas, dahlias, salvias and kangaroo paw, *Anigozanthus flavidus*, adds to the exotic appearance of the garden.

For the time being, the original climbing roses still grow against the Kitchen Garden wall, but eventually there are plans to replace them with the Chilean bell flower, *Lapageria rosea*, which has proved to be hardy elsewhere in Gloucestershire. Among the rarities in this garden is the Tasmanian Huon Pine, *Lagarostrobus franklinii*, which is one of the slowest-growing trees in the world. At 50 years old its trunk has reached a modest 4 inches in diameter. Nearby, a specimen of the unusual Chilean shrub *Vestia foetida* is best admired at a distance; both its attractive yellow flowers and its foliage are described as "malodorous". Beneath the shrubs and trees, a wonderful fern, *Blechnum tabulare*, forms dense carpets of waist-high fronds.

The garden is tidied up in the Spring and given a top-dressing of compost and, although it looks rather shell-shocked after this treatment, it soon recovers. Any new plantings incorporate the organic fertilizer, fish, blood and bone, into the soil to help the plants establish quickly.

The only contrived aspect of the Southern Hemisphere Garden is the wrapping of the tree ferns and bananas to protect them during the Winter months, but this treatment has made it possible to keep them growing at Highgrove. Now that these plants are well established, rarer specimens are being added as David Howard uses his previous experience in botanical gardens to spot unexpected plants in interesting places, or to collect botanical material from which he can raise plants. The experimentation continues.

# The Azalea Walk

UNTIL FAIRLY RECENTLY, this long narrow garden between two walls was more of an access corridor to the Walled Garden than a place of year-round interest in its own right. It consisted of a pathway between two strips of grass on which were arranged a series of large terracotta pots containing fragrant azaleas.

Then, three years ago, Prince Charles suggested that this part of the garden could become more interesting if the planting were made three-dimensional. As part of this process, an "architectural rescue" stone doorway was incorporated into the Eastern wall with the help of garden designers Julian and Isabel Bannerman, and this now leads through to the Arboretum. The doorway was carved with natural images and enigmatic hieroglyphs by students from the Prince's Institute of Architecture. It is topped by busts of people the Prince considers as "Worthies": Dame Miriam Rothschild, Dr Kathleen Raine, The Dowager Duchess of Devonshire, Sir John Tavener and, most recently, Dr Vandana Shiva. As this was an area that had always been difficult to mow, the gardeners were pleased to be asked to become involved with its redevelopment.

*Tender ferns grow between the terracotta pots that contain specimen azaleas. The Azalea Walk is very sheltered, yet gets no more than three hours of sun daily, providing ideal conditions for the ferns.*

This entrance to the Arboretum features carvings by students of the Prince's Institute of Architecture.

This memorial to Prince Charles's much-missed fox terrier Tigga is set into the Azalea Garden wall.

In any garden, if the gardeners share in the decision-making they feel a sense of ownership that helps hold a project together and move it forward. Too often they don't get asked. Ideally, design projects should involve the gardeners at the earliest stage; they can then contribute to its development and take charge once the builders leave.

In the Azalea Walk, the grass borders were removed and replaced with a collection of tender ferns from Australasia, South Africa and Taiwan. As this area of the garden gets no more than three hours of sun daily, it is a perfect place to grow ferns. Even *Cyathea dregei*, a rare South African tree fern from the Drakensberg Mountains, has survived through several British Winters. Climbers had already been added to soften the walls and although the terracotta pots remain in their original positions, the Prince planted clematis in with the azaleas to extend the season of interest.

What had previously been an area which looked rather austere for much of the year has now become a special feature of Highgrove and the garden of three-dimensional beauty envisaged by Prince Charles.

# Beginning an Organic Garden

*"Since 2001 and the loss of my beloved grandmother, some new aspects of gardening have presented themselves. The garden at Clarence House was in itself somewhat similar to other neighbouring gardens, so in 2002 I set about changing certain aspects of it. The idea was never to remove the original garden, but to enhance it and rekindle the evolutionary processes which make a garden dynamic."*

HRH THE PRINCE OF WALES

# Clarence House

WHEREAS HIGHGROVE IS a garden entirely of the Prince's own devising, both Clarence House in London and Birkhall in Scotland are gardens which previously belonged to his grandmother, the late Queen Elizabeth. While honouring the memory of his much-loved grandmother, Prince Charles has gradually begun to make his own mark since taking over these gardens. Changes are subtle and sensitive; some practical, for easier maintenance and to bring the gardens under organic management, and some reflecting the Prince's different taste in plants.

Although considerably larger than average, Clarence House has to deal with many of the problems that beset any city garden. It is next to a busy road, with its attendant noise and pollution; there are fewer natural predators to deal with pests; and, together with all London gardeners, Prince Charles must use water responsibly. With this in mind, the possibilities of installing a rainwater harvesting system are currently being explored.

The garden extends over approximately half an acre. It is a mixture of formal and informal areas and is dominated by a pair of magnificent London plane trees, *Platanus* x *hispanica*, set in a wide expanse of lawn. In Spring, the grass beneath the trees is studded with clusters of naturalized daffodils and snakeshead fritillaries. On warm days throughout the Summer this is a favourite place for the Prince to hold alfresco events and meetings.

Directly outside the portico of Clarence House, Prince Charles has created a new garden in memory of his grandmother. The aim was both to "frame" the house and to create a short vista leading the eye from the long corridor on the ground floor of the house out through the front door and into the garden beyond. It is a formal garden, with York stone paving slabs forming central, cross-shaped

*A York stone path, edged with box and planted with varieties of creeping thyme, leads to the sundial at the centre of the Rosicrucian Garden that Prince Charles has created in memory of his grandmother.*

ABOVE AND BELOW: *The unusually shaped dawn redwood is a deciduous conifer which turns a eye-catching bronze in Autumn and then drops its needles. In Spring, the tree is covered in a haze of fresh green growth.*

paths and narrower gravel paths running between the box-edged borders. The stone slabs were laid on a bed of sand to allow the spaces between them to be planted with creeping thymes. The borders are planted with lavender 'Imperial Gem' and the dark red rose 'The Prince', with seasonal plantings of deep blue salvias in Summer and pansies in Winter.

Four standard evergreen oaks, *Quercus ilex*, lend height and structure to the garden and a row of four more is planted in the border across the path from the parterre. At the centre point of the garden, where the main paths cross, there is an elegant sundial surrounded by box. The box has been planted to create the outline of a York rose, representing the time when Prince Charles's grandmother was Duchess of York. Its name, the Rosicrucian Garden, is a play on the words "rose" and "cross" and it is a garden rich in symbolic meaning for the Prince.

Against the hedge that screens the garden from The Mall there is a raised area that dates back to the 17th century, when it was part of a promenade around three sides of the garden. The raised walks to the East and West no longer exist, while the surviving walk has become a 300-foot long herbaceous border, fronted by a grass bank which slopes downwards towards the lawn. In the late Queen Elizabeth's time there was a wooden platform at the back of the border from which the Royal Household could observe processions. The border had become seriously infested with bindweed so needed updating and this was done by digging up all the plants and painstakingly removing every scrap of bindweed root. As the bindweed was also growing among the roots of the hedge, a trench was dug and a barrier was installed to prevent any recolonization. With an empty, weed-free border, Prince Charles could redesign this area; the platform has gone and the border is now deeper, with a generous scalloped edge at the front to allow additional planting. This creates the impression that the plants are tumbling down the bank and into the garden. Its length is divided at intervals by yew hedging, which will be clipped into stepped yew buttresses once it has matured.

The new planting is in shades of pink, purple, blue and white and incorporates many of the Prince's favourite plants, particularly buddleias and Old English roses, including 'Eglantyne', 'Cordelia', 'Sceptr'd Isle' and 'Marinette'. These

TOP: *Tepees of runner beans are planted behind the delphiniums at the rear of the long border.*

ABOVE: *The new planting uses many of Prince Charles's favourite flowers in pinks, purples, blues and white. Buddleias, Old English roses, delphiniums and hostas are much in evidence.*

ABOVE LEFT: *The beds in the Rosicrucian Garden are planted with 'Imperial Gem' lavender and the dark red Old English rose 'The Prince'.*

LEFT: *Spring bulbs in flower beneath a blossom-laden crab apple tree on the main lawn.*

are inter-planted with eupatorium, lithrum, *Hydrangea arborescens* 'Annabelle', *H. paniculata* 'Grandiflora' and *H. quercifolia* 'Pee Wee', and the tall *Salvia guaranitica* 'Argentine Skies' as well as some runner bean tepees. Towards the front of the borders, lower-growing plants include prunella, *Heuchera* 'Prince', *Alchemilla mollis*, and *Salvia patens* 'Chilcombe', which dies down over Winter but comes back reliably each year in this sheltered border.

Now that this planting is well established, work has started on the next phase, which extends the border along the full length of The Mall wall, adding two further bays, again divided by yew buttresses. As soon as the layout is complete they will be planted using the same palette and plant selection.

Ornamental trees are a major feature of the garden. Some are very old, including an exceedingly old pear tree and a black mulberry, *Morus nigra*, that is reputed to have been planted in the time of James I, although Mark Lane, the Head Gardener from Buckingham Palace, has his doubts. The flowering trees include a pair of very tall limes, several magnolias, crab apples, a foxglove tree, *Paulownia tomentosa*, and the handkerchief tree, *Davidia involucrata*.

There are advantages as well as disadvantages to gardening in the centre of a city. The temperature is markedly higher here at Clarence House, which means that tender plants need less cosseting than at Highgrove. Even the unwelcome air pollution has the beneficial effect of keeping the roses free of many diseases that can be a problem in cleaner air. Mildew has been a problem in the past, but regular applications of a humus-rich organic soil conditioner – such as Moorland Gold (see The Blueprint, page 164) – and attention to good air circulation seem to have helped with this.

In theory, the visiting ducks from St James's Park should be rootling around the borders gobbling up the slugs and snails, but they are probably too well fed to make the effort. Instead, Mark employs a Soil Association Approved garlic product which is used both as a spray and as granules (see The Blueprint, page 164). This is applied every six weeks and has proved very effective. Asked what the product smells like, Mark's response is, "Unbelievable! But it does subside after an hour or so." He has also found that it is effective against greenfly. Bio-fuels are used for all the garden machinery and Mark has observed that this too creates an interesting smell in the garden. There is, he says, a distinct air of the fish and chip shop when they are in use.

Mark explains, "In general terms, care of this garden is no different from any large suburban London garden. We keep the edges tidy, mow the lawns, dead-head in Summer and leaf-sweep in the Autumn." The only difference is that it is all managed organically. "When we knew the Prince was going to move in we immediately began the conversion to organic systems. For example, we bought the weed-burner in advance of his arrival so that we could stop using weedkillers on the paths." Central to the management of the garden are the regular deliveries of Highgrove manure to improve and feed the well-drained soil, which is prone to drying out. Pea sticks also come from Highgrove and are used to support the plants in the herbaceous borders in as natural a way as possible.

ABOVE AND BELOW: *The late Queen Elizabeth, The Queen Mother, planted many ornamental trees, including this delicate flowering cherry (above). Prince Charles is now adding new trees to the garden, such as the standard evergreen oaks in the Rosicrucian Garden.*

*The shrub borders are under-planted with Spring bulbs which will be followed by shade-tolerant perennials later in the year. The white star-shaped flowers of ipheion will be followed by bluebells, and as they die back, hardy geraniums take over.*

*Lavender 'Imperial Gem' is one of the best deep blue lavenders. It grows into a neat mound that does not split open as the plant ages.*

At present there isn't a suitable place in the garden for making either compost or leaf mould, so, for the time being, this is carried out in the Buckingham Palace gardens. Although the Palace gardens are increasingly adopting environmentally friendly practices they are not yet organic, so plans are underway to incorporate a recycling centre into the garden at Clarence House. This will be at the far end of the main path and will be concealed behind a pair of decorative gates. Finding a suitable spot in the garden for composting is a dilemma Prince Charles shares with most gardeners. Ideally it should be easily accessible or it will not be fully used; however, compost heaps or bins are not attractive and need some concealment. A gated enclosure, a hedge or even a group of shrubs can shield them from the rest of the garden without making them inaccessible.

Like many other urban gardeners, Prince Charles has begun to consider the benefits of giving over some of his London garden to growing fruit and vegetables. An area is being prepared as a formal potager with box-edged beds and standard rosemary bushes. The beds will be planted with salads and herbs. If this proves successful, a larger area will be developed as a potager. In a move that in some ways harks back to the "Dig for Victory" campaign of the Second World War, Prince Charles would like to lead by example and encourage city residents, wherever feasible, to grow at least some of their own food, be it in a garden, an allotment, or even on a balcony or rooftop.

With climate change, international instability and the looming shortage of fossil fuels, there is an increasing danger that urban food supplies will not remain as reliable as they are today. Growing and sourcing food locally introduces a measure of stability and has knock-on beneficial effects. Householders or local councils can compost all their green waste and return the fertility to the soil, while reducing landfill. Gardens and allotments become oases for the beneficial wildlife which helps to keep pests under control.

For the gardener, gardening is a healthy activity and is generally far more productive and satisfying than a visit to the gym. Perhaps most importantly of all, children become aware of where food comes from – not from supermarket shelves, but from the earth, which must be cherished if it is to continue to feed them and future generations. And, of course, home-grown fruit and vegetables cannot be bettered for freshness – and lack of food miles.

New gardeners should start with something easy; a single 10-inch pot of rocket leaves will add spice to salads over many weeks and encourage further experiment. Equally, a large pot of alpine strawberries will prove undemanding

*Magnolias were the favourite trees of Prince Charles's grandmother and there are many fine specimens in the Clarence House gardens. The flowers range in colour from white and palest pink to deep magenta.*

RIGHT: *Snakeshead fritillaries, with their intriguing chequerboard flowers, have naturalized successfully in the damper areas of the lawn. They are left undisturbed until they have set seed to allow them spread and multiply.*

*A specimen of the Chinese shrub* Pseudopanax davidii. *A rare plant that is found in very few gardens, it was planted in the Clarence House garden in 1996.*

and be surprisingly productive. Don't be too ambitious at the beginning or there is a danger that you may lose heart if you fail. Pots, filled with organic potting compost, are a good starting point. It is a way to familiarize yourself with the basic techniques of seed sowing, planting and caring for crops in a controlled environment. Pests such as slugs and snails are also easier to spot and remove.

The soil in urban gardens can be of extremely poor quality and is often unsuitable for growing food crops without a great deal of improvement. A solution to this problem is to create raised beds and fill these with a mixture of bought-in good-quality soil and compost (preferably home-made). Like pots, raised beds are a more controllable environment in which to grow food plants. They should be positioned in a sunny sheltered part of the garden and can be simple constructions of timber boards nailed to corner posts. The local cats – and foxes – will make a beeline for the beds, so it is advisable to use cloches or netting until the plants are large enough to deter visitors. You will also need to be vigilant against smaller pests, especially slugs and snails. Throwing them into an adjoining garden is not neighbourly and is also ineffective as they have a homing instinct. The garlic spray recommended by Mark Lane will act as a deterrent, or you could treat the area with nematodes.

Not all gardens are suitable **for growing** food crops; they may face North or be shaded by trees or buildings. If **this is the c**ase, find out if there are any allotments nearby and visit them to see if **anyone is int**erested in sharing a plot. A full plot can look very large and daunting **to the ine**xperienced gardener, especially if it is covered in weeds, and some sit**es have leng**thy waiting lists. Not only will sharing a plot be less intimidating, it w**ill also give** you time to assess whether you want, or need, a full plot and to learn **about gard**ening from the other plot holders. Most of them will be very happy to **pass on surp**lus young plants, spare seeds and their invaluable expertise. Some of **the older** gardeners may still be enthusiastic users of chemical fertilizers and pest**icides, but** allotment holders are becoming increasingly organic. (See The B**l**ueprint, page 164 for details of how to find an allotment near you.)

*"A similar story is to be told at Birkhall, in Scotland, where a larger garden in a similar condition, although with a wholly different climate, needs the same breath of life to rekindle those dynamic aspects. My darling wife has a keen eye for this garden and also for the cutting garden, from which she conjures exquisite flower arrangements. Sharing in this evolutionary process of natural gardening is a pleasure that I would encourage all who read this book to undertake."*

HRH THE PRINCE OF WALES

# Birkhall

BIRKHALL IS THE MOST PRIVATE of the Prince's gardens. Set on the edge of the Balmoral Estate in the Scottish Highlands, it is a much-loved home, visited as often as possible by Prince Charles and the Duchess of Cornwall. There is a relaxing sense of informality about it, reflecting that this is where they go to spend time alone or with family and friends. Their other homes also serve as offices, venues for entertaining and receptions, and in the case of Highgrove, a visitor attraction which sees more than 25,000 people pass through its gates annually as it raises funds for the Prince's charities. Here, there isn't the same pressure to keep everything immaculate; changes can take place gradually and no one need be overly concerned about a weedy border.

This is fortunate for Caroline Mathias, Birkhall's main gardener, as the climate here means that doing any gardening at all can be challenging at times. In Winter, the sun is so low that once the frost comes into the garden it stays and the ground remains frozen. It is not unusual to lose roses from the cold. Although Great Britain is a relatively small country, there are wide climatic variations and what you grow and when you plant must take local conditions into account, with general advice adjusted accordingly. Looking at neighbouring gardens is often the most useful guide to what plants will grow in the locality and when tasks should be carried out.

When Caroline first arrived at Birkhall six and a half years ago she had great plans for taking all the plants out of the borders and reorganizing and replanting them during the Winter months. But when faced with long periods of permafrost

*The lower, productive garden is known as The Bell because of its shape. It is in the most sheltered, South-facing part of the garden where it gets the maximum amount of sunshine.*

*The Bell is a typical Scottish garden with its mixture of flowers, fruit and vegetables. The kaleidoscopic effect of the planting is most evident when the garden is viewed from the terraces in front of the house.*

she soon realized this wasn't going to happen. While still working for the late Queen Elizabeth, she concentrated instead on maintaining the status quo as best she could. Once Prince Charles took over, however, they began to plan the replanting of the borders. The Prince agreed that with so short a growing season, she could start this reorganization in October each year, while he and the Duchess are still in residence.

Because Birkhall was also a garden which had previously belonged to his grandmother, the Prince wished to be respectful of how she had developed it over many years, while introducing changes and additions. Converting the garden to organic management was quite straightforward, requiring only that they stopped using weedkiller on the paths. "You do have to adopt a more relaxed approach to weeds," Caroline acknowledges. "We are still sorting out how best to look after the driveways. We purchased a flame burner but it has never been very effective at Birkhall, owing, I think, to the wet Springs. Highgrove and Clarence House certainly use them to greater effect."

As with Clarence House, some recent changes are for practical reasons. A good example of this is the towering cypress hedge that used to divide the garden from the main entrance. Although it was a valuable windbreak, keeping it trimmed involved getting a crane (for health and safety reasons) sent from Glasgow, resulting in a £1,000 bill for ten minutes' work. An attractive stone wall has replaced it, topped with heather thatch that in turn has a turf ridge where wild flowers grow. The turf is given a trim in Winter and watered during the Summer.

The wall incorporates an extremely elegant pavilion at its far end – a memorial to the late Queen Elizabeth – with windows overlooking the entire garden and the views beyond. It is a place where Prince Charles and the Duchess can enjoy the garden while sheltered from the prevailing, and often chilly, wind.

The garden slopes steeply away to the South, with woodland surrounding the house on its other three sides. In the wooded areas of the garden, nesting boxes and feeders for birds and red squirrels are much in evidence, reflecting that this is a garden where Prince Charles has the opportunity to spend time observing the natural world.

On the Southern side, the borders, which are tucked up against the house, now have permanent plantings of Spring bulbs. Growing narrow-leaved bulbs such as narcissi, grape hyacinths and *Chionodoxia*, prevents the foliage smothering the young herbaceous plants that follow. These herbaceous plants need no staking because they are cut back in June to delay flowering until August, when Prince Charles and the Duchess are at Birkhall. Timing is crucial; Caroline has found that if they haven't been cut back by the 2nd or 3rd of June, they won't flower that year. This is a technique that can be usefully employed in any garden to delay

*Prince Charles has replaced an overlarge and rather gloomy cypress hedge with this heather-thatched, turf-ridged wall. His own design, the wall is an equally effective windbreak and far more pleasing in appearance.*

*There are bird tables and feeders throughout the gardens. Keeping them filled is a regular task that Prince Charles, an avid birdwatcher, undertakes when he is staying at Birkhall.*

flowering for a special event, or to extend the flowering season of a clump of plants by selectively pruning them so that not all will flower at once.

Against the house, *Buddleia davidii* has been trained as an unusual wall shrub. Its branches are kept trimmed and every month or so during the growing season its exuberant new growth is cut back until eventually it is allowed to flower in late August. The front of the borders is lined with Autumn crocus, *Colchicum autumnale*, which has attractive, dense foliage early in the year; this dies back in midsummer (when the house is not occupied) and is replaced by a haze of the lilac-shaded flowers in Autumn. In front of the borders, the grass edging has been replaced with stones to save time that used to be spent keeping the edges neat.

To the West, a stone wall curves round to meet the house, almost mirroring the new wall at the other end. The random niches within the wall have led to speculation that it may have been used to display auriculas. Caroline has found it difficult to persuade anything to grow in these niches because they are so dry. This quality was recently exploited by her dogs when she was working in the border on a very wet day – she looked up to find that each had selected a niche and curled up in it to keep themselves dry. Above this wall, there is a small hillock

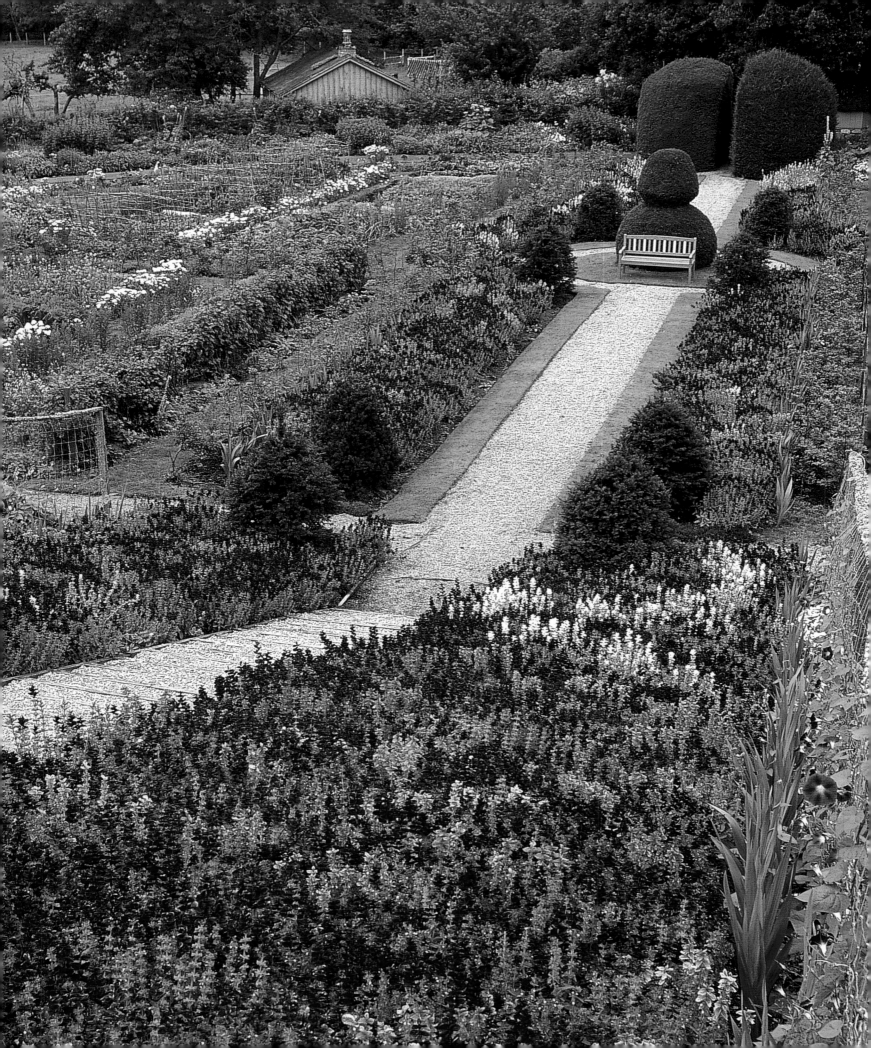

LEFT: *Dramatic bands of vibrant clary sage,* Salvia horminum, *in shades of blue, pink and white, line the steps that lead down to The Bell and then border the main path that leads through the garden.*

ABOVE: *Looking up from the herbaceous borders in The Bell towards the Eagle's Nest gazebo. The flowers are regularly cut for the house which tempers the plants' growth and means they don't need dividing as frequently.*

crowned by the Eagle's Nest, a heather-thatched gazebo which perches at the highest point in the garden.

From the lawn in front of the house, the garden slopes steeply down to a terrace and then again to the lower, productive garden which is known, because of its shape, as The Bell. As with his other gardens, Prince Charles is happy to have lawns that consist largely of moss. Caroline comments, "This is fortunate because if you live within a mile of the Dee, you have moss."

The apples and plums trained against the terrace walls are at least a hundred years old. Birkhall is just within the limits of altitude at which apples can be grown successfully. It is too high, however, for blackberries and blueberries, neither of which ripen here unless grown under glass. The ground beneath the apples and plums is thickly planted with nerines. These Autumn-flowering bulbs add a vivid splash of brilliant pink in October and are an invaluable addition to the Duchess's flower arrangements, which fill the house whenever she is at Birkhall. The borders at the front of the Terrace are planted with the deep red rose 'Europeana' and edged with alpine strawberries and heather. Self-seeded violas have been left to grow among the roses and have now been joined by a planting of dark blue

*The Duchess of Cornwall fills the house with flowers cut from the garden when she is staying at Birkhall. The Prince and their guests are great admirers of her informal arrangements.*

pansies. The rose bushes are showing their age and, although they are wonderful for cutting, their stems have a tendency to flop to the ground and break in heavy wind or rain, so Caroline is looking for a replacement. If nothing significantly better is found, they will propagate from the old plants, since this rose is no longer available commercially.

In the late Queen Elizabeth's time, the borders on either side of the steps leading down from the Terrace to the lower garden were traditionally planted with phlox. They were badly affected by mildew, however, and looked unsightly by the end of the season so they have now been replaced by a colourful annual planting of clary sage, *Salvia horminum*, with lavender-pink gladiolus 'Royal Dutch'. These are set against a backdrop of dark blue and dark red morning glories which twine through the rustic trellises at the back of the borders.

On the grassy slope below the terrace, the initials ER (Elizabeth Regina) and CP (Charles Princeps) are elegantly outlined in box as another memorial to Queen Elizabeth from her grandson. Box does well at Birkhall; it does go very yellow in late Winter and early Spring, but then recovers quite quickly. Prince Charles spent part of his honeymoon helping to plant the box. Caroline reveals that both the Prince and the Duchess spent a great deal of their honeymoon finding homes for the many plants they were given as wedding presents and they did much of the planting themselves.

The Bell is essentially a productive kitchen and cutting garden, where flowers, soft fruit and vegetables are intermingled in a traditional Scottish manner. From August to October little is bought in and this garden supplies much of the fruit and vegetables, as well as all the cut flowers for the Duchess's arrangements.

Changes are happening here too, but they are adjustments rather than anything major. Prince Charles has added yews that will be topiarized for Winter structure and he is considering planting box hedging to provide a framework for the lower garden. The crops have changed too, with fewer potatoes and more soft fruit to fit in with modern tastes.

Practical measures have also been taken to make this area less labour intensive. Caroline has a small team of helpers and must use their time as efficiently as possible. Aside from her two assistants, who work with her for one day a week, she also has the help of a local farmer three days weekly during the Summer. A good example of one of the successful time-saving measures that have been introduced are the paths within The Bell. Gravel paths used to run between the beds and because their management was particularly time-consuming they became increasingly weedy. To control this, Caroline started to mow them and they have gradually become grass paths instead.

Either side of the main path on the far side of The Bell, there is an attractive pair of matching duck houses, although one is kitted out with beds for Caroline's dogs. It seems that the Indian Runner ducks and dogs understand and respect their individual territories. The ducks have made a big difference to the garden, freeing Caroline from the task of picking slugs and snails off cabbages. These ducks were an introduction by the Prince, who has a particular fondness for these highly amusing and idiosyncratic birds.

It is impossible not to smile when the Indian Runner ducks come into view. They are the corps de ballet of the Birkhall garden, appearing all in a line, stage left, with their heads held high, pausing only briefly to gobble up a slug or two before exiting stage right. They seem so purposeful, seldom loitering around in the manner of ordinary ducks and certainly never waddling. Their lives are conducted at a brisk pace as they run in formation, quacking all the while, from one spot to another.

There is a long history of keeping Indian Runner ducks in Scotland. From the middle of the 19th century, merchants imported them from Southeast Asia (the islands of Indonesia, not India), because they were prodigious egg layers. This quality was valued since they could be crossed with domestic breeds to improve

*The opportunistic Indian Runner ducks check around the bird table to hoover up any seed the Prince might have spilt when he was topping up the feeders. They regularly arrive on the lawn in time for afternoon tea.*

ABOVE: *The ducks provide invaluable slug control, patrolling through the borders and rootling out every juicy morsel. Since their arrival at Birkhall, the gardeners have noticed far less slug damage.*

BELOW: *A side channel of the River Muick flows past the bottom of the Birkhall garden, necessitating a barrier to prevent the ducks from disappearing upstream.*

the latter's productivity. Their extraordinary upright gait led to them originally being named Penguin Ducks; hazy geography then led to the name Indian Runner.

With its unusual shape, The Bell is well suited to a somewhat higgledy-piggledy layout, with short rows and blocks of seemingly random planting of vegetables among soft fruit canes and stands of herbaceous plants. It adds to the informality and charm of this garden, which sits so comfortably in its beautiful setting alongside the River Muick, within the wider landscape of small pastures, wooded hills and glens.

All waste from the garden and kitchen is composted, but with such a small team it isn't practical to make compost in the quantities or as intensively as at Highgrove, so good-quality well-rotted cattle manure is also used. This is particularly important for ground preparation, as the manure, along with seaweed extract and poultry manure, helps the very free-draining sandy and acidic soil to retain moisture and nutrients. As for the compost heaps, Caroline explains, "We build two a year. The compost is built up in layers, as and when material comes off the garden. Everything is put on the heap – kitchen scraps, grass clippings (every two weeks during the cutting season), weeds and herbaceous clippings. Once the bin is full, we cover it and leave it for six months, then turn it with a pitchfork. It is then covered with a carpet and left for another six months until the process is

*The productive garden supplies fresh, seasonal organic vegetables to the house each day when Prince Charles and the Duchess of Cornwall are in residence.*

*The carrot crop is protected from damage by sowing a rootfly-resistant strain of seed and covering the crop with fine netting (Enviromesh). Enviromesh can also be used to keep cabbage-white butterflies off brassicas.*

complete. Although this compost is not as rich in nutrients as the Highgrove mix, the use of manures compensates for this."

Weeds such as chickweed, bindweed and ground elder have invaded some of the borders. Caroline knows that they will have to be tackled at some point, but until she has the time to dig everything up, she controls the weeds by pulling out the foliage. Due to the short growing season and the constant picking, the herbaceous plants in the borders don't clump up quickly and need dividing only every five years instead of the more usual three. Wholesale weed removal will be left until a border is due for this treatment. This is the best course of action in most gardens: where weeds are not choking out more desirable plants they are best tolerated until they can be tackled properly. In future, wherever possible, a weed-suppressing membrane will be laid when the borders are renewed. Holes will be cut for planting and the membrane will then be disguised with a mulch. This will eliminate much of the weed problem and make the garden less labour intensive.

*Gardener Caroline Mathias, hoes one of the gravel paths. This used to be far more time consuming, but in recent years the minor paths in The Bell have been allowed to grass over and can be mown instead.*

*A fine crop of brassicas is corralled behind home-made willow fencing. These decorative touches add to the charm of what might otherwise be a utilitarian part of the garden.*

Birkhall Winters are too cold for many of the common pests to survive from year to year, and, with the good wild bird population and the slug-hunting ducks, most of the pests that do survive are controlled naturally. Enviromesh (a fine netting) is used to cover carrots and brassicas to prevent damage by carrot root fly and cabbage white butterflies. With both these pests, prevention is better than cure – there is no treatment for root fly once it has attacked a carrot crop, and hand-picking caterpillars off brassicas can be a laborious business. Fortunately, deer are not a problem in the garden, but despite the gardeners' best endeavours, rabbits do seem to get in.

Diseases are kept at bay using preventative methods. In the flower borders the foliage of *Alchemilla mollis* is cut back in June, both to encourage fresh leaves and to keep the plants free of mildew. In the Bell, mildew can also be a problem on gooseberry and currant bushes; to prevent this the fruit is thinned as it forms to ensure good air circulation.

Another important method of disease prevention, as in any organic garden, is crop rotation. At Birkhall the vegetables are planted in small blocks rather than rows and are interspersed with blocks of flowers to attract beneficial insects.

*Prince Charles and Caroline discuss the day's gardening tasks. The Prince and the Duchess are very hands-on in Birkhall's gardens. They even spent part of their honeymoon finding homes for the many plants they had received as presents.*

*Birkhall is the most personal and informal of the three gardens, a place where Prince Charles and the Duchess of Cornwall can relax away from their royal duties and enjoy free time with family and friends.*

6

The Blueprint

# 1: The Essential Elements

## Soil biology

Plant health is intimately linked to soil biology. In fertile soils, plant roots interact with bacteria and fungi in the most extraordinary way, exuding sugary "sap" through their root hairs. These provide nourishment for the soil organisms, which in turn break down humus, releasing nitrates and other plant nutrients in an absorbable form.

Such "balanced" nutrition enables plants to manufacture a range of complex organic compounds which could be loosely described as the plant's immune system. When attacked by insects or fungal spores plants mobilize these substances, such as phenolic compounds and caffeic acids, to help them resist disease or pest damage. These are not only what give plants their characteristic smells and flavour but also the healthiest components of fruit and vegetables!

Research has shown that plants that are nourished organically, rather than through soluble chemical fertilizers such as nitrate and super phosphate, contain higher levels of these health-promoting compounds.

## Compost

Recipes for Highgrove's experimental compost mix: sieve leaf mould, loam and compost as required (see proportions below), to remove lumps. Mix thoroughly. Store the mix in a black bin bag or a dustbin if it is not to be used immediately.

FOR SEEDS AND CUTTINGS

1 part leaf mould

1 part sand

FIRST POTTING

4 parts leaf mould

2 parts loam

1 part grit

MATURE PLANT MIX

4 parts leaf mould

5 parts loam

4 parts garden compost

2 parts grit

½ part blood, fish and bone (optional)

## Woodchip mulch

Woodchip is used as an aesthetic mulch when planting trees to simulate forest floor conditions. After each tree is planted, it is surrounded by 5 square yards of weedmat or old carpet, which is then topped by a 6-inch layer of woodchip. Not only does the weedmat/carpet conserve moisture, it also separates the mulch from the soil so that it does not use up available nitrogen as it decomposes. (This happens in woodland, where rain and bacteria start the slow rotting process.) At Highgrove they have used all types of carpet successfully, but they do not recommend the foam-backed varieties. Carpet tiles work well and once the fibre has decomposed the rubber backing can be recycled. Wool is 10–11 per cent nitrogen, so fleece can also be used as an old-fashioned and excellent mulch. In the days when the woollen mills were still a major industry, shoddy was an important slow-release fertilizer for gardeners.

After four to six years, the woodchip mulch will have rotted down and any nutrient will have washed into the soil by rain. During that time the mulch has kept the soil moist and the root zone has been protected from perennial weeds. By year six, a tree will cast sufficient shade to inhibit weeds and it has been given the best start, with no competition, plenty of moisture and a bit of feed.

## Woodchip-fired heating system

As nearly all the Highgrove Estate's trees have now been planted, there will be limited use for mulch in the future. (It isn't used on the borders because it would deplete the soil of nitrogen.) Instead, the 20 tons of woodchip produced annually by the estate will be used to fire a new heating system. An augur feeds the woodchip on to a burner no larger than a hand and a thermometer controls the rate at which the augur delivers the woodchip. This system uses 96 per cent of the energy in the woodchip and is smokeless. Every ton burned produces a single bucket of ash which is returned to the woodland. This system has been in use in Finland for 50 years. The only energy used is the diesel to run the woodchipper, but it is hoped that this will be bio-diesel in the future. In every way possible, Highgrove is moving away from the use of petrol.

## *Flowforms*

A flowform is a man-made cascade which simulates the action of a mountain stream by leading the water downwards through specially shaped bowls in a rhythmic pattern. This both aerates the water and enhances its ability to support the organisms that are needed for biological water cleaning. Flowforms are available in the United Kingdom from IRIS WATER (tel: 01287 660002; website: www.iriswater.com) and in the USA from FLOWFORMS USA (website: www.flowformsusa.com).

# 2: The Productive Gardens

## *Walled Garden seed list*

BEETROOT
'Chioggia' – a traditional sweet-flavoured Italian variety which reveals pink and white stripes when cut open
'Boltardy' – traditional variety, good for early sowing

BROAD BEANS
'Super Aquadulce' – suitable for Autumn sowing
'Bunyards Exhibition' – a Victorian variety
'Imperial Green Longpod' – suitable for Autumn sowing

BRUSSELS SPROUTS
'Brilliant' $F_1$ – early variety, with good disease resistance
'Trafalgar' $F_1$ – tall, sweet-flavoured variety that crops from December to late January, so good for Christmas

CABBAGE
'Spitfire' $F_1$ – pointed cabbage that can be harvested from May to June
'January King' – one of the best for Winter use

CARROTS
'Nantes 2' – a sweet early carrot
'Sugarsnax' – sweet with a high beta-carotene content
'Kinbi' $F_1$ – bright yellow in colour
'Starca' $F_1$ – stores well
'Berlicum' – a high quality red/orange maincrop variety

CHARD
Swiss Chard – green spinach-like leaves and thick white stems that can be cooked as a separate vegetable
Rhubarb Chard – with bright red leaves
Rainbow Chard 'Bright Lights' – highly decorative with green, pink, yellow and red leaves
Bright Yellow Chard

COURGETTES
'Defender' – very early, with regular shaped fruit which are produced all Summer if cropped regularly; resistant to cucumber mosaic virus

FRENCH BEANS
'Montano' – heavy crops of pencil-thin pods: good disease resistance
'Maxi' – beans carried above leaves; resistant to bean mosaic virus

LEEKS
'Alcazar' – blue-green variety
'Startrack' – early, long and slim
'Swiss Giant-Zermatt' – early, long and slender with moderate rust resistance

LETTUCE
'Little Gem' – baby cos-type lettuce with sweet flavour
'Saladin' – classic iceberg with mildew and leaf-rot resistance
'Vienna' – Spring to Autumn cropping iceberg; resistant to mildew and aphids (they don't like the flavour)

ONION SETS
'Sturon' – large golden bulbs

PEAS
'Early Onward' – one of the earliest to crop
'Balmoral' – late-cropping variety
'Cavalier' – sweet-flavoured maincrop; resistant to powdery mildew
'Onward' – superbly flavoured with a heavy crop
'Greenshaft' – wonderful flavour early maincrop; resistant to downy mildew and *Fusarium* wilt

POTATOES
'Arran Pilot' – first-early, oval shaped with white skin and flesh with firm waxy texture
'Desiree' – maincrop with pink skin, yellow flesh and excellent flavour; it is drought resistant and keeps well, but is prone to scab
'Pink Fir Apple' – knobbly, late-maturing variety with yellow flesh and a very good texture and flavour

RUNNER BEANS
'Painted Lady' – good variety with decorative red and white flowers
'Desirée' – slender bean of exceptional flavour

SPINACH
'Giant Winter' – very hardy, stands well with lance-shaped, fleshy leaves
'Matador' – Summer variety that is slow to bolt and very tasty
'Viroflay' – an extremely vigorous "monster" spinach

TOMATOES
'Super Sweet F100' – a cherry tomato with long trusses of very sweet tomatoes that are high in Vitamin C

'Shirley' $F_1$ – an outstanding variety for greenhouse cultivation with delicious flavour and excellent disease resistance

## *Pruning fruit trees*

For advice on pruning fruit trees, look at *Fruit & Vegetable Gardening*, published by Dorling Kindersley for the RHS, or *Pruning and Training Plants* by David Joyce, published by Mitchell Beazley.

## *WRAGS*

The WOMEN RETURNERS TO AMENITY GARDENING SCHEME (WRAGS) provides practical hands-on training to women who wish to work in horticulture. Trainees each work 15 hours a week in a carefully sourced garden under the instruction of the garden owner or head gardener. Contact WRAGS for more information (tel: 01285 658339 or website: www.wfga.org.uk).

## *Cutting Garden seed list*

*Amaranthus caudatus* – red and green
*Anethum graveolens* 'Mariska'
*Asclepias incarnata* 'Soulmate'
Canterbury bell 'Champion Blue' and 'Champion Lavender'
Cosmos 'Seashells'
Cynoglossum 'Mystery Rose'
Gourd – small fruited form
*Jasione perennis* 'Blue Light'
Larkspur – 'Sublime Special Mixed'
Lupin 'Sunrise'
*Moluccella laevis*
Nicotiana – 'Perfume Blue', 'Lime Green', 'Bright Rose' and 'White'
*Nigella damascena* 'Persian Jewels
*Nigella orientalis* 'Transformer'
*Physostegia virginiana* 'Crown of Thorns' and 'Grandiflora Rose'
*Salvia horminum* 'Monarch Mixed'

Stock Miracle 'Mixed' and 'Forcing Wonder' Mix
Strawberry Corn 'Zea'
Veronica 'Sightseeing'

## Cutting Garden – fillers and foliage

Cerinthe, *Cerinthe purpurescens*
Clary sage, *Salvia sclarea*
Solomon's seal, *Polygonatum x hybridum*
Rosemary
Mint
Myrtle, *Myrtus communis*
Pussy willow, *Salix caprea*

## Cutting Garden – flowers

SARAH'S TULIP SELECTION:
'Queen of Night' – it's always good to be able to echo what's
    in the garden when I choose material for the house
'Maureen' – lovely tall leggy platinum blonde of a tulip;
    creamy ivory and perfect for cutting
'Angélique' – pale pink double
'Apricot Beauty' – as lovely as it sounds
'Prince Charles' – of course!
'Menton' – china rose
'White Triumphator' – lily-flowered tulip
'Spring Green' – ivory turning to green
'Carnival de Nice' – white striped with red
'Ballerina' – flamed blood red on lemon background;
    inside marigold orange and red
'Black Parrot' – large and blousy with frilly edge
'Abu Hassan' – dark mahogany, yellow edge
'Ivory Floradale' – ivory yellow, slightly spotted with
    carmine
'Bruine Wimpel' – lavender pink, feathering to a brownish
    orange edge
'Maytime' – reddish violet, narrow white edge
'Black Hero' – double 'Queen of Night'
Assorted parrot tulips, plus pot-planted early tulips such
    as 'Christmas Marvel' (satin pink), 'Christmas Dream'
    (rich rose pink) and 'Coquette' (white)

PEONIES
'Sarah Bernhardt' – double ruffled pink
'Duchesse de Nemours' – double ruffled white
'Sea Shell' – single, mauve-pink
'Lotus Queen' – white, with yellow centre
'Karl Rosenfeld' – crimson, globe-shaped with inward
    curving petals

OTHERS
Cosmos
Bleeding Heart, *Dicentra spectabilis*
Foxgloves, *Digitalis purpurea albiflora*
Snapdragons, *Antirrhinum*
Pinks, *Dianthus* 'Mrs Sinkins'

## Pests and disease control

SOME GENERAL ADVICE
Crop rotation: do not grow the same crop in a bed two years
in a row, to cut down on pest and disease problems.

The use of home-produced compost and potting mixtures
reduces the risk of imported soil-borne diseases.

Natural predators such as birds, wildlife and beneficial
insects are primary pest controllers. Allow chickens to
scratch around in an orchard and they will deal with the
bugs. They can also be let loose in the vegetable garden,
but only in the Winter or on cleared beds or they will
eat the plants.

For serious insect infestations try Eradicoat, a starch-based
organic insecticide. Available from DEFENDERS (tel: 01233
813121; website: www.defenders.co.uk).

SPECIFIC PROBLEMS AND REMEDIES
Apple canker – prune it out, remembering to clean secateurs
    or pruning saw afterwards to prevent spreading the
    disease.
Blackfly – pick off affected shoots and crush under foot.

Box blight – cut out and remove all infected stems and leaves. Aim to open up the centre of the hedge for good air circulation and shape hedges so that they shed, rather than hold, water.

Carrot root fly – grow resistant varieties such as Resistafly, protect with Enviromesh or sow in late July.

Deer – install deer-proof fencing or move.

Flea beetle – plant brassicas in light or partial shade.

Gooseberry mildew – grow 'Invicta', which is resistant to mildew and plant bushes at least 4 feet apart to promote good air circulation.

Gooseberry sawfly – check for caterpillars and hand-pick them off the bushes before they get out of hand.

Greenfly – a good population of birds and ladybirds will control greenfly. If you do have problems use the *Aphidius colemani* wasp, which parasitizes aphids, for plants under glass; outdoors, spray with a jet of water or garlic spray.

Honey fungus – there is no organic way of stopping the progress of honey fungus, but if caught early, it can be contained by using mushroom compost as a mulch. A fungus in the compost will attack honey fungus when it encounters it, slowing and containing its progress.

Mealy bug – introduce the natural predator *Cryptolaemus montrouzieri* (Australian ladybird).

Red spider mite – keep humidity high under glass by spraying paths with water and introduce the natural predator *Phytoseiulus persimilis* (a predatory mite).

Rabbits – netting, 3 feet above ground and buried at least 12 inches below ground level, is the only solution

Rose diseases – replace old varieties that are disease-prone with modern, resistant varieties; mix roses with other plants to avoid build-up of rose diseases; remove and burn all disease wood and leaves.

Slugs and snails – for plants under glass, use nematode products such as Nemaslug or Slugsure; outdoors: hand-pick them late in the evening or after rain; use nematodes, beer traps, garlic spray or granules; ducks, hedgehogs, slow worms, frogs and toads all feed on slugs and snails.

Vine weevil – the vine weevil nematode has proved 100 per cent successful at Highgrove.

Whitefly – introduce the natural predator *Encarsia formosa* (wasp); for a serious infestation, coat a piece of cardboard with petroleum jelly and run it over the plants – the whitefly will fly up and stick to it.

BIOLOGICAL PEST CONTROLS ARE AVAILABLE FROM:

AGRALAN tel: 01285 860015; website: www.agralan.co.uk

DEFENDERS tel: 01233 813121; website: www.defenders.co.uk

THE GREEN GARDENER tel: 01603 715096; website: www.greengardener.co.uk

SCARLETTS tel: 01206 242530; website: ww.scarletts.co.uk

WIGGLY WIGGLERS tel: 01981500391; website: www.wigglywigglers.co.uk

## *Fruit varieties*

BROGDALE HORTICULTURAL TRUST is home to the National Fruit Collection with more than 2,300 varieties of apple, 550 of pear, 350 of plum, 220 of cherry and 320 varieties of bush fruits. Contact on 01795 535286; email: info@brogdale.org; website: www.brogdale.org

# 3: The Ornamental Gardens

## *Carpet Garden*

There have been a number of changes to the planting since the Carpet Garden was moved to Highgrove, all designed to make it easier to manage and reduce the number of plants needing Winter protection. However, the six potted citrus trees have been retained; when they flower they fill the garden with their fragrance and contribute to the exotic atmosphere. As do other tender specimens that include the coral tree *Erythrina crista-galli*; *Nerium oleander*; the pomegranate *Punica granatum*; *Tibouchina*; *Abutilon* 'Thompsonii' and *Sparrmannia africana*. In the Summer they are plunged, still in their pots, into the borders. The cork oak, *Quercus suber*; olive, *Olea europaea*; and tamarisk, *Tamarix*, are permanently planted into the garden and have settled happily into their new surroundings, surviving through the Winter. Elsewhere hardier plants have replaced the exotic planting: Hydrangea 'Merveille Sanguine' (literal translation Bloody Marvellous), with its rich plum-coloured flowers, has proved a great find, while two deep red, intensely fragrant climbing roses 'Guinee' and 'Etoile de Hollande' have superseded the tender climbers. The "carpet" that spreads across the middle of the garden is planted with a combination of English roses, 'Falstaff', 'Gertrude Jekyll', 'Louise Odier', 'Prince Charles' and 'Ferdinand Pichard', accompanied by the silver foliage of *Artemisia schmidtiana* 'Nana' and the vibrant reddish-purple colouring of *Berberis thunbergii* 'Atropurpurea Nana'.

## Growing thymes

Mediterranean-type herbs, such as varieties of thyme, lavender and rosemary can be tricky to grow in the UK for a number of reasons. In the wild they survive in the poorest of soils in full sun and with very little water. Rich, moisture-retentive soil rots their roots, especially in Winter when they hate to be cold and wet. This is not helped by most commercially raised herb plants being grown in a soil-less potting medium. It is essential to soak them thoroughly before they are planted and gently to loosen the rootball or the compost will form a non-absorbent plug around the plant and the roots will have difficulty making their way into the surrounding soil. If this happens, instead of drowning the plants will desiccate and die.

Herbs that have been raised in a gritty, soil-based potting medium will transplant more successfully. One of the most successful ways to establish creeping herbs among paving stones is to mix the seed with a loam-based seed compost and brush it into the cracks between the stones.

## Roses

Contact details for DAVID AUSTIN ROSES – tel: 01902 376300; website: www.davidaustinroses.co.uk

## Platonic and Archimedean Solids

The following description is by Professor Keith Critchlow. The five Platonic Solids represent the unfolding of a sphere with 4, 6, 8, 12 or 20 sides. It is more accurate to call these "figures" as they can be outlines as well as solids. In the Platonic set there are what are generally known as the five Regular Platonic Figures. These all have equal edge lengths and equal faces. Plato did not reveal the details of the Dodecahedron or even name it. He describes these regular geometric figures as "molecules" of Fire (Tetrahedron), Air (Octohedron), Water (Icosahedron) and Earth (the Cube, or Hexahedron). He implied that there was no need to explain the nature of a "certain other figure" (Dodecahedron) as "the friends of the Gods" would know it anyway. The conclusion is that Plato was under oath as a member of the Pythagorean Mathematical Society not to reveal its details. Thus there is ample reason for Prince Charles, in semi-poetical or semi-philosophical mode, to hide the greater part of the Dodecahedron.

In contemporary science, the four elements as described in Ancient Greece are now called "states of matter": Fire is "radiance", Air "gaseousness", Water "liquidity" and Earth "solidity". In essence these are identical to those of the Ancient Greeks. The difference being that for the ancient sages the original elements were deeply symbolic and not just definitions of physical states. Fire was the spiritual dimension of light, Air the intellectual dimension (Divine as well as Human), Water, the emotional, or feeling, dimension and Earth the physical sensory dimension. The Archimedean "figures" all have edges of equal length and, like the Platonic figures, sit within a containing sphere with all points or corners touching the sphere's surface. However, the Archimedean figures have different but regular faces, although they are all truncations of the Platonic figures and all can be derived from the Tetrahedron. There are 13 in total, of which the truncated Tetrahedron is central.

These Figures, the forms and unfolding of "Sacred Geometry", are the archetypes of two- and three-dimensional space upon which are built all further natural forms and figures. For more information read *Order in Space* by Professor Critchlow, published by Thames & Hudson.

# 4: The Informal Gardens

## *Tulip fire*

Symptoms include fungal spores that infect emerging shoots. These develop malformed leaves and may shrivel and rot; in damp weather they may be covered with grey fungal spores. Other symptoms are brown spots on the leaves and flowers, which may also rot, and flowers may topple if stalks are attacked. To control tulip fire, remove diseased plants immediately and destroy them (don't put them in the compost heap). Do not plant tulips in this area for two years. Only plant healthy looking, undamaged bulbs and lift and discard bulbs each year.

## *The National Council for the Conservation of Plants & Gardens*

THE NATIONAL COUNCIL FOR THE CONSERVATION OF PLANTS & GARDENS (NCCPG) seeks to conserve, document, promote and make available Britain and Ireland's biodiversity of garden plants for the benefit of everyone through horticulture, education and science. Tel: 01483 211465; website: www.nccpg.com

## *Ferns*

BRITISH PTERIDOLOGICAL SOCIETY is a forum for fern enthusiasts. More details are available on their website: www.nhm.ac.uk

# 5: Beginning an Organic Garden

## *Moorland Gold*

Moorland Gold is a by-product of the water industry. Water pouring off mountainsides naturally picks up particles of peat which collect in filters before the water enters the reservoirs. This has not been mined and the peat moors are left untouched for wildlife to flourish. It can be used in place of conventional peat. Available from THE ORGANIC GARDENING CATALOGUE – tel: 0845 1301304; website: www.organiccatalog.com

## *Garlic barrier*

Various makes of garlic barrier are available by mail order from:
HARROD HORTICULTURAL – tel: 01502 505300; website: www.harrodhorticultural.com
GREENFINGERS – tel: 0845 3450728; website: www.greenfingers.com
GARLIC BARRIER (USA) – website: www.garlicbarrier.com

## *Allotments*

Local councils usually manage a number of allotment sites and will have up-to-date information on availability/waiting lists. A standard allotment plot is 300 square yards.
The average rent is £25, although rents vary from as little as £3 per year to £70.
Alternatively, contact the NATIONAL SOCIETY OF ALLOTMENT AND LEISURE GARDENERS LTD on 01536 266576; website: www.nsalg.org.uk

# Birkhall seed list

## VEGETABLES

Beetroot – 'Boltardy', 'Burpees Golden', 'Chioggia'

Broad bean – 'Imperial', 'Green Windsor', 'Stereo', 'Meteor'

Broccoli – Mixed

Brussels sprout – 'Nelson', 'Maximus', 'Falstaff'

Calabrese – 'Arcadia'

Cardoon

Carrot – 'Resistafly', 'Amsterdam Maxi', 'Purple Haze'

Cauliflower – 'Aviron'

Courgette – 'Bambino', 'Yellow Bird'

Dwarf French bean – 'Nassau', 'Purple Queen'

Florence Fennel – 'Rudy'

Kale – 'Black Tuscany', 'Redbor'

Kohl rabi – 'Kolibri'

Leek – 'Jolant'

Lettuce – 'Little Gem', 'Pandero', 'Saladin'

Mooli – 'April' Cross

Mustard – 'Red Giant', 'Spicy Green' Mix, 'All Greens' Mix, Braising Mix

Parsnip – 'Avonresister'

Pea – 'Feltham First', 'Hurst Green Shaft', 'Sugar Snap'

Phacelia – green manure

Potato – 'Epicure', 'Red Duke of York', 'Desiree', 'Juliette', 'Pink Fir Apple', 'Sarpo Axona'

Rocket – 'Discovery'

Runner Bean – Dwarf 'Hestia'

Salsify – 'Giant'

Savoy cabbage – 'Capriccio'

Scorzonera – 'Russian Giant"

Swede – 'Invitation'

Swiss chard – 'White Silver', 'Bright Lights'

Turnip – 'Purple Top Milan', 'Market Express'

## HERBS

Borage

Chervil – curled

Coriander

Dill

Parsley – plain-leaved, Bravour

Tarragon

## FLOWERS

*Achillea millefolium* – 'Cerise Queen', 'Cassis'

*Agrostemma atrosanguinea*

*Ammi visnaga*

*Androsace* – 'Stardust'

Antirrhinum – 'Sonnet', 'Madame Butterfly'

*Asarina antirrhinifolia*

Aubretia – blue

*Bupleurum griffithii*

Calendula – 'Touch of Red'

Candytuft

Carthamus – 'Shiro'

*Centaurea moschato* – 'Dairy Maid'

Commelina – 'Sleeping Beauty'

Cornflower – 'Blue Boy', 'Florence Blue', 'Florence Violet'

Cosmos – 'Pied Piper'

Delphinium – x *bellamosum*, 'Zalil', 'Magic Fountain Midnight'

Echium – 'Blue Bedder'

*Erinus alpinus*

Godetia – F$_1$ 'Grace' Mix

Gypsophila – 'Silverstar'

Harebell

Hollyhock – 'Queeny' Mix, 'Nigra'

Ipomoea – 'Clarks Heavenly Blue', 'Scarlett O'Hara', 'Grandpa Ott', *purpurea* 'Kniola's Black Knight', 'Star of Yelta',

Larkspur – 'Bright Carmine', 'Dark Blue', 'Gentian Blue', 'Cloudy Skies', 'Moody Blues'

Limonium – 'Stardust'

*Linum grandiflorum* – 'Blue Dress'

*Malva sylvestris* – 'Zebrina', 'Mystic Merlin'

*Matthiola bicornis* – night-scented stock

Nasturtium – 'Empress of India' (tall single-flower climber), 'Black Velvet', 'Gleaming Mahogany'

Nemophila – 'Penny Black'

Pansy – 'Fancy Purple'

Papaver – 'Pacino', 'Angels Choir', 'Black Paeony'

*Pardanthopsis dichotoma*

Parthenium – 'Butterball'

Penstemon – 'Giant Mix'

Polemonium – 'Blue Pearl

Salpiglossis – 'Royale Chocolate'

Salvia – 'Salsa Plum', *horminum* blue, rose, white, *lyrata* 'Purple Volcano'

*Scleranthus biflorus*

Statice – apricot, dark blue, rose, white

Stock – 'Miracle Mix', 'Legacy Mix'

Sunflower – 'Prado Red'

Sweet Pea – 'Cupid Mix'

*Verbena rigida* – 'Polaris'

Wahlenbergia – 'Melton Bluebird'

## Tools

The tools at Highgrove are carefully maintained implements, some of which have already seen a lifetime's use by two or three owners. An example of this is David Howard's border fork which was manufactured by Isaac Ash in 1890 and is a model of perfection which he fully expects to pass on in due course. Clasp its wooden shaft just above the metal sleeve and it will balance perfectly on the palm of one hand. Neither end is too heavy or too light because the craftsman who made it understood how to combine steel and wood to make a balanced garden instrument. Bad balance is a sign of poor design. Should the wooden shaft eventually break, it will be replaced, although many of the tools in the shed still have their original handles.

Tools are always cleaned before they are put away and oiled if they are not due to be used for some weeks. All tooled steel rusts unless it is stainless steel.

The old craftsmen understood the importance of a tool being solid-forged from one piece of steel. Cheap modern tools are welded together from separate pieces and have inherent weaknesses. Recently, inspired by the quality of the old tools, Prince Charles and David Howard have commissioned a range of Duchy Original stainless steel garden tools. They went to the traditional maker Caldwells whose logo, dating from 1900, proudly says "Best in the World". The new tools are not cheap, but the idea is that they should last a lifetime and beyond. Provided, of course, that they are treated with respect. This includes never using a fork or spade as a lever – a crowbar should be used instead. In time, should the wooden handle break, as with the antique tools, it should be taken to a specialist repairer to be properly rebalanced. Your local WOODLAND TRUST (tel: 01476 581135; website: www.woodland-trust.org.uk) is a good starting point to find such a craftsman in your area.

Other tools in regular use are a mixture of the old and the new. Practicality, rather than sentimentality, governs the choice of the right tool for the job and sometimes new tools for specific functions are a decided improvement on the old. As is the case with the modern, lightweight razor pruning saw with an extending handle and the Lazy Dog weeding tools for removing deep-rooted weeds (LAZY DOG TOOL COMPANY, tel: 01751 417351; website: www.yark.co.uk).

Some machinery is essential to help with maintenance of the gardens. There is a policy of replacing it regularly to keep up with reduced exhaust emissions and improved fuels. All larger pieces run on diesel so that they can, as soon as practical, be run on bio-diesel. Chainsaws, hedgetrimmers and brushcutters, which traditionally run on highly polluting two-stroke petrol, are now fuelled by Aspen, an alkylate petrol that is expensive, but kinder to the environment. Aspen is available from HUSQVARNA machinery dealers (website: www.husqvarna.co.uk).

*The Duchy Collection of gardening tools are designed to last a lifetime or longer – like the vintage forks and spades that are in daily use in the gardens at Highgrove.*

# Highgrove Calendar

## January

Garden project – a major project is carried out each year during the Winter months, the most recent being the replanting of the Lily Pond Garden.

Hazel coppicing to produce staking material for the garden and sufficient material to make tepees, arches and bean poles.

Rose pruning of the Pergola and the arbours in the Walled Garden.

Willow cutting, wholesale cut so that the wood may be sufficiently dried in order to use for weaving in February/March.

Spread manure on vegetable beds and rotavate when the weather allows.

Chit (sprout) potatoes to get them off to an early start and improve the crop.

Start sowing annuals, half-hardy and tender perennials in the heated glasshouse.

Sow early crops of spinach, celery and carrots in cold frames in the middle of the month.

## February

Garden project (as above).

Hazel coppicing (as above).

Cut back herbaceous borders, lightly fork soil and mulch beds and borders with garden compost.

Rose pruning – remaining bush roses and climbers in the remainder of the garden.

Remove old foliage from strawberries in Model Fruit Garden.

Winter-prune apple and pear trees.

Start sowing Cutting Garden annuals and biennials under glass.

## March

Completion of garden project(s).

Making woven plant supports from willow and hazel for immediate use in the garden.

Mowing, giving lawns first cut, edging.

Continue cutting back herbaceous borders, lightly fork soil and mulch beds and borders with garden compost.

Plant sweet pea tunnel in Walled Garden.

Mulch fruit bushes in Model Fruit Garden with manure or compost.

Main sowing of annuals, half-hardy and tender perennials in the glasshouse.

Potato planting.

Mulch comfrey with compost to keep it productive.

Rotavate wildflower verges.

Continue sowing Cutting Garden annuals and biennials under glass.

## April

Plant annuals and tender half-hardy perennials in the Walled Garden borders.

Fill gaps in borders in Ornamental Gardens, replacing failed plants or changing if a plant hasn't performed well or there is a colour clash.

Start direct sowing of vegetables, including spinach, beetroot and peas, in the Walled Garden.

Plant out tomatoes in the glasshouse.

Continue sowing Cutting Garden annuals and biennials under glass.

Start direct sowing Cutting Garden annuals with fortnightly sowings of clary sage and love-in-a-mist.

Stake herbaceous plants.

Unwrap tree ferns and bananas in the Southern Hemisphere Garden as the danger of severe frost should have passed.

Weeding.

## May

Plant up plots with Summer schemes.

Stake herbaceous plants.

Stake and support flowers in the Cutting Garden.

In cold frames, plant out cucumbers and sow basil.

Dead-head and cut back plants after they have flowered to extend their season.

Continue direct sowing Cutting Garden annuals with fortnightly sowings of clary sage and love-in-a-mist.

## June

Commission the ornamental water feature in the Carpet Garden.

First cut of beech hedge.

Move pots of citrus and other associated plant material from glasshouses to Carpet Garden.

Stake and support flowers in the Cutting Garden.

Dead-head and cut back plants after they have flowered to extend their season.

Continue direct sowing Cutting Garden annuals with fortnightly sowings of clary sage and love-in-a-mist.

## July

Clipping of box in Walled Garden and Sundial Garden.

Complete clearing of Meadow and mow to give lawn-like effect.

Cut meadow, regardless of what has and has not flowered.

Harvesting of acid cherries, early raspberries.

Make hay or silage, depending on weather conditions.

Late sowing of carrots to avoid rootfly.

Prune cherry trees as soon as they finish fruiting.

Harvest first early potatoes.

## August

Clip yew topiary and hedges.

Harvest damsons and plums.

Harvest maincrop potatoes.

Trim lavenders when they have finished flowering.

Take cuttings of tender plants, e.g salvias, near the end of the month.

Summer-prune trained fruit trees in Model Fruit Garden and the Walled Garden.

Take a critical look at the garden while it is at its peak and decide on the next Winter project.

## September

Cut yellowing asparagus foliage close to the ground, weed and dress with well-rotted manure or compost.

Mow wildflower verges.

Start to tidy and cut back in the Cutting Garden.

Plant bulbs in the Cutting Garden.

Clip hornbeams (stilt hedges).

Clip *Quercus ilex* topiary.

Harvest early apples.

Second clip of beech hedges.

## October

Harvest late apples and pears, including crab apples to make crab apple jelly.

Winterize the Carpet Garden, drain the water feature and protect mosaic from frost damage.

Wrap up tree ferns and bananas in the Southern Hemisphere Garden with straw and hessian to protect from Winter frost.

After foliage is knocked back by frost, dig up the dahlias and store in a frost-free place over Winter.

Dig up chocolate cosmos in Cutting Garden, pot up and keep in the glasshouse over Winter.

Clear annuals from Cutting Garden.

Plant bulbs in Cutting Garden.

Harvest pumpkins and ornamental gourds.

## November

Garden project started; in 2005 this was the new sandstone entrance pillars and the new Buttress Garden.

Leaf raking throughout all areas of garden.

Plant Spring bulbs in open ground and pots.

Tree planting in the garden and on the estate.

Cut Autumn-fruiting raspberries to the ground.

Lightly prune Cutting Garden roses.

## December

Garden project continues.

Leaf raking throughout all areas of the garden.

Boxing Day – Dennis starts vegetable seed sowing in heated greenhouse.

Take woody cuttings of shrubs that have become too large or need increasing.

# Acknowledgements

THE AUTHORS WOULD LIKE TO THANK all of those who have helped on this book. Particular thanks must go to David Howard (Head Gardener), David Wilson, Jane Battersby, Jess Usher, Sarah Champier and Dennis Brown at Highgrove; Mark Lane (Head Gardener at Buckingham Palace); Gilbert Harris (Clarence House); Caroline Mathias (Head Gardener at Birkhall), and to all other garden and estate staff. We would also like to thank Virginia Carington, Elizabeth Buchanan, Leslie Ferrar, Siobhan Brooks, Catie Bland and Margaret Walker for their tremendous support; also Professor Keith Critchlow (for advice on Sacred Geometry); Emma Clark (for advice on The Carpet Garden); and Patrick Holden, Craig Sams and Kate Langrish for their advice on the manuscript. Thanks, too, to Andrew Lawson, David Rowley, Susan Haynes, Nigel Soper and Jinny Johnson for their help and encouragement in the production of this book.

# Index

NOTE: All garden areas mentioned are at Highgrove unless otherwise specified. The seed and plant listings in the Blueprint, and the Calendar, have not been indexed. Page numbers in italics refer to photographs.

First published in Great Britain in 2007
by Weidenfeld & Nicolson

10 9 8 7 6 5 4 3 2 1

Text copyright © A.G. Carrick Limited, 2007
Design and layout © Weidenfeld & Nicolson 2007

Photography by Andrew Lawson

All chapter opener photographs were taken by David Rowley at Birkhall in Summer 2006.

Additional photography by David Rowley (pages 2, 19, 36, 37 top left, 41, 42, 56 bottom, 69, 84 bottom, 100, 134, 135 top, 135 bottom, 136 top, 136 bottom, 137 top, 137 bottom, 138 top, 138 bottom, 139 top, 139 bottom, 140, 141 top, 141 bottom, 142, 145, 148-9, 150, 151 bottom, 154, 155, 172, front endpaper, back endpaper).

Photographs on pages 20 and 56 top left, by Kevin Lomas.

Illustration on pages 12-13 by Robbie Polley.

All rights reserved. No part of this publication may be reproduced, stored in a retrieval system, or transmitted, in any form or by any means, electronic, mechanical, photocopying, recording or otherwise, without the prior permission of both the copyright owner and the above publisher.

The right of the copyright holders to be identified as the authors of this work has been asserted in accordance with the Copyright, Designs and Patents Act 1988.

A CIP catalogue record for this book is available from the British Library.
ISBN-13: 978 0 297 84416 7
ISBN-10: 0 297 84416 4

Printed and bound in Italy

The Orion Publishing Group's policy is to use papers that are natural, renewable and recyclable products and made from wood grown in sustainable forests. The logging and manufacturing processes are expected to conform to the environmental regulations of the country of origin.

Design director David Rowley
Editorial director Susan Haynes
Designed by Nigel Soper
Edited by Jinny Johnson
Design assistance Justin Hunt and Joanna Cannon
Proofread by Gwen Rigby
Index by Elizabeth Wiggans

Weidenfeld & Nicolson
The Orion Publishing Group Ltd
Orion House
5 Upper St Martin's Lane
London WC2H 9EA
www.orionbooks.co.uk